普通高等院校"十三五"艺术与设计专业系列教材

艺术设计专业英语

明 兰 主编

清华大学出版社
北京交通大学出版社
·北京·

内容简介

本书内容包括艺术设计史、设计专题、设计大师、中国艺术、设计教育五大板块。每个板块内又包括几课,每课由背景知识、课文、词汇、注释和练习组成,文章中穿插大量精美图片,图文并茂,对于拓展学生的专业知识和信息量大有裨益。最有附有练习参考答案和参考译文供读者参考,有助于帮助读者提高阅读艺术设计类文献的水平。

本书条理清晰,文字简明易懂。

本书可作为高等艺术院校艺术设计专业的教材,也可作为广大艺术设计工作者和艺术设计爱好者的参考资料。

本书封面贴有清华大学出版社防伪标签,无标签者不得销售。
版权所有,侵权必究。侵权举报电话:010-62782989　13501256678　13801310933

图书在版编目(CIP)数据

艺术设计专业英语 / 明兰主编. --北京 :北京交通大学出版社 :清华大学出版社,2011.9(2025.2 重印)

(普通高等院校"十三五"艺术与设计专业系列教材)

ISBN 978-7-5121-0705-2

I. ① 艺⋯　II. ① 明⋯　III. ① 艺术–设计–英语–高等学校–教材　IV. ①H31

中国版本图书馆 CIP 数据核字(2011)第 170067 号

艺术设计专业英语
YISHU SHEJI ZHUANYE YINGYU

责任编辑:	韩素华	特邀编辑:周志杰		
出版发行:	清 华 大 学 出 版 社	邮编:100084	电话:010-62776969
	北京交通大学出版社	邮编:100044	电话:010-51686414
印　刷　者:	北京虎彩文化传播有限公司		
经　　　销:	全国新华书店		
开　　　本:	185 mm×260 mm　印张:10.5　字数:259 千字		
版　　　次:	2011 年 9 月第 1 版　2025 年 2 月第 8 次印刷		
书　　　号:	ISBN 978-7-5121-0705-2/H•248		
印　　　数:	8 301～8 600 册　定价:28.00 元		

本书如有质量问题,请向北京交通大学出版社质监组反映。对您的意见和批评,我们表示欢迎和感谢。
投诉电话:010-51686043,51686008;传真:010-62225406;E-mail:press@bjtu.edu.cn

前言 Preface

本书是一本实用的艺术设计类专业英语教材。全书取材广泛，分为艺术设计史、设计专题、设计大师、中国艺术、设计教育五大板块。艺术设计史板块介绍了工艺美术运动、国际主义平面设计风格等设计流派的特征及其代表人物；设计专题板块覆盖面广，内容包括平面设计、产品设计、环境艺术设计、动漫设计、服装设计、多媒体设计等各方面的专业知识；设计大师板块可以使学生了解各个设计领域杰出设计师的生平及代表作品；中国艺术板块介绍了中国画及民间美术等独具特色的内容；设计教育板块主要介绍国外著名设计院校的特色。教师可根据学习期间的专业课程设置和教学内容，有选择地运用本书，使所选课文与正在学习的专业课程内容相一致。

为了增强学生学习的兴趣和积极性并便于教学，每个单元都由课文、背景知识、词汇、注释和练习组成，书中还加入了大量精美图片，图文并茂，有助于拓展学生的专业知识和信息量。本书最后附有练习参考答案和参考译文供读者学习时参考，有助于读者提高阅读艺术设计类文献的水平。

本书旨在使学生具备运用英语从事专业阅读、专业翻译和专业交流的综合能力，并在提高艺术修养的同时，增加艺术专业英语词汇量，以期对他们将来在国际艺术领域的进一步学习和探索有所帮助。本书为设计艺术类专业英语教材，可作为高等院校艺术设计相关专业学生的专业英语教材使用，也可供从事相关专业的人员学习参考。

本书在编写过程中得到了同事们的大力支持与帮助，在此表示真诚的感谢。感谢谢沁沁、周芬芬老师参与了资料的收集工作，感谢李晖老师在图片处理工作中所做出的努力，感谢闫洁峰、刘峰老师后期的校对工作，他们的付出和努力为本书的编写提供了很大的帮助。

由于编者水平所限，书中难免有不妥和错误之处，恳请各方有识之士批评指正。

明 兰

2011年9月6日

艺术设计专业英语

目录 Contents

Unit One History of Art and Design 1

Lesson 1 Arts and Crafts Movement 2
Lesson 2 Art Nouveau 7
Lesson 3 Constructivism 12
Lesson 4 Bauhaus and the Education of Design 16
Lesson 5 The International Typographic Style 21

Unit Two The Special Topics About Design 25

Lesson 6 Corporate Identity 26
Lesson 7 Book Designer Fiona Raven 30
Lesson 8 Successful Industrial Design 34
Lesson 9 IDSA 39
Lesson 10 Environmental Design 44
Lesson 11 Famous Interior Designers and Their Styles in Interior Design 49
Lesson 12 How to Become a Fashion Designer 54
Lesson 13 The History of Animation 59
Lesson 14 The History of Photoshop 64
Lesson 15 Dreamweaver and It's Advantages 70

Unit Three Design Masters 73

Lesson 16 World Graphic Design Master: Paul Rand 74
Lesson 17 Raymond Loewy — the Man Who Streamlined the Sales-Curve 80

Lesson 18	Frank Lloyd Wright and His Architectures	86
Lesson 19	Fashion Queen — Coco Chanel	91
Lesson 20	Hayao Miyazaki's Movie World	96

Unit Four   Chinese Art ... 101

Lesson 21	Landscape Painting in Chinese Art	102
Lesson 22	Chinese Folk Art	107
Lesson 23	Eric Chan — Finding Balance in Design	112

Unit Five   Design Education ... 117

| Lesson 24 | Birmingham Institute of Art and Design | 118 |
| Lesson 25 | Savannah College of Art and Design | 123 |

参考答案 ... 127

Lesson 1	Arts and Crafts Movement	128
Lesson 2	Art Nouveau	128
Lesson 3	Constructivism	128
Lesson 4	Bauhaus and the Education of Design	128
Lesson 5	The International Typographic Style	128
Lesson 6	Corporate Identity	128
Lesson 7	Book Designer Fiona Raven	128
Lesson 8	Successful Industrial Design	129
Lesson 9	IDSA	129
Lesson 10	Environmental Design	129
Lesson 11	Famous Interior Designers and Their Styles in Interior Design	129
Lesson 12	How to Become a Fashion Designer	129
Lesson 13	The History of Animation	129
Lesson 14	The History of Photoshop	129
Lesson 15	Dreamweaver and Its Advantages?	130
Lesson 16	World Graphic Design Master: Paul Rand	130
Lesson 17	Raymond Loewy — The Man Who Streamlined the Sales-Curve	130
Lesson 18	Frank Lloyd Wright and His Architectures	130
Lesson 19	Fashion Queen — Coco Chanel	130
Lesson 20	Hayao Miyazaki's Movie World	131
Lesson 21	Landscape Painting in Chinese Art	131
Lesson 22	Chinese Folk Art	131
Lesson 23	Eric Chan — Finding Balance in Design	131

Lesson 24　Birmingham Institute of Art and Design 131
Lesson 25　Savannah College of Art and Design 132

参考译文 133

第1单元　艺术设计史 134
第2单元　设计专题 137
第3单元　设计大师 150
第4单元　中国艺术 157
第5单元　设计教育 160

Unit One

History of Art and Design

Lesson 1　Arts and Crafts Movement

'Have nothing in your houses that you do not know to be useful, or believe to be beautiful.'
　　　　　　—William Morris'The Beauty of Life',1880

　　The Arts and Crafts Movement was an international design movement that originated in England and flourished between 1880 and 1910, continuing its influence up to the 1930s. Instigated by the artist and writer William Morris (1834–1896) in the 1860s and inspired by the writings of John Ruskin (1819–1900), the movement advocated truth to materials and traditional craftsmanship using simple forms and medieval, romantic or folk styles of decoration, against the styles that had developed out of machine-production.

William Morris　　　　　　　　　　　　　John Ruskin

　　The movement was influenced by Ruskin's social criticism, which sought to relate the moral and social health of a nation to the qualities of its architecture and design. Ruskin thought the machine was at the root of many social ills and that a healthy society depended on skilled and creative workers. Like Ruskin, the Arts and Crafts artists tended to oppose the division of labor[1] and to prefer craft production, in which the whole item was made and assembled by an individual or a small group. They were concerned about the decline of rural handicrafts, which accompanied the rise of industry, and they regretted the loss of traditional skills and creativity.

　　In fact, the Arts and Crafts style[2] was in part a reaction against the style of many of the things shown in the Great Exhibition of 1851[3], which were ornate, artificial and ignored the qualities of the materials used. The art historian Nikolaus Pevsner[4] has said that exhibits in the Great Exhibition showed 'ignorance of that basic need in creating patterns, the integrity of the surface' and 'vulgarity in detail'. Design reform began with the organizers of the Exhibition itself, Henry Cole (1808–1882), Owen Jones (1809–1874), Matthew Digby Wyatt (1820–1877) and Richard Redgrave (1804–1888). Jones, for example, declared that 'Ornament ... must be secondary to the thing decorated', that there must be 'fitness in the ornament to the thing ornamented', and that wallpapers and carpets must have no patterns 'suggestive of anything but a level or plain'. These ideas were taken up by William Morris. Where a fabric or wallpaper in the Great Exhibition might be decorated in a natural motif made to look as real as possible, a William Morris wallpaper, like the artichoke design illustrated below, would use a flat and simplified natural motif. In order to express the beauty inherent in craft, some products were deliberately left slightly unfinished, resulting in a certain rustic and robust effect.

Wallpaper designed by Morris

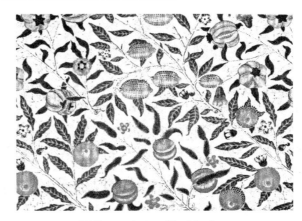
Wallpaper designed by Morris

By the end of the 19th century, Arts and Crafts ideals had influenced architecture, painting, sculpture, graphics, illustration, book making and photography, domestic design and the decorative arts, including furniture and woodwork, stained glass, embroidery and weaving, jewelry and metalwork.

Starting from 1855, the Association continuously held a series of exhibitions in England to provide the public with a good opportunity to understand the design and elegant design taste, so as to promote the movement. Widely exhibited in Europe, the Arts and Crafts Movement's qualities of simplicity and honest use of materials inspired designers like Henry van de Velde [5] and movements such as Art Nouveau[6], Vienna Secession[7], and eventually the Bauhaus[8]. Pevsner regarded the movement as a prelude to Modernism, which made use of simple forms without ornamentation.

Background Information

Arts and Crafts Movement：工艺美术运动是起源于19世纪下半叶英国的一场设计改良运动，其产生受艺术评论家约翰·拉斯金和建筑师普金等人的影响，参考了中世纪的行会制度。运动的时间大约为1859—1910年，得名于1888年成立的艺术与手工艺展览协会。其起因是针对装饰艺术、家具、室内产品、建筑等因为工业革命的批量生产所带来设计水平

下降而开始的设计改良运动。

John Ruskin：约翰·拉斯金（1819—1900），英国作家、艺术家、评论家，工艺美术运动理论的奠基者。

William Morris：威廉·莫里斯（1834—1896），杰出的诗人、文学家、画家，英国工艺美术运动的倡导者，从事绘画、玻璃、陶器、家具、书籍装帧等各方面的工作。

Words and Expressions

1. originate [ə'ridʒineit] *vt.* 发起，发明　*vi.* 发源，来自，产生
2. flourish ['flʌriʃ] *vi.* 茂盛，繁荣
3. instigate ['instigeit] *vt.* 教唆，怂恿，煽动，鼓动
4. inspire [in'spaiə] *vt.* 鼓舞，激发；赋予……灵感
5. advocate ['ædvəkeit] *vt.* 提倡，主张
6. craftsmanship ['krɑːftsmənʃip] *n.* 技术，技艺
7. criticism ['kritisizəm] *n.* 批评，批判，指责；评论，评论文章
8. relate to 涉及，与……有关
9. architecture ['ɑːkitektʃə] *n.* 建筑，建筑学，建筑物
10. at the root of 根源，起源
11. tend to 易于，往往会，倾向于
12. assemble [ə'sembəl] *vt.* 集合，收集；装配，组装
13. rural ['ruːrəl] *adj.* 乡村的，农村的，田园的
14. in part 在某种程度上，部分地
15. ornate [ɔː'neit] *adj.* 装饰华丽的，过分装饰的
16. artificial [ˌɑːtiˈfiʃəl] *adj.* 人工的，人造的，假的；矫揉造作的，虚假的
17. pattern ['pætən] *n.* 花样，图案；样品，样本
18. integrity [in'tegriti] *n.* 完整，完全；正直，诚实
19. vulgarity [vʌl'gæriti] *n.* 粗俗，庸俗，粗鄙
20. ornament ['ɔːnəmənt] *n.* 装饰，装饰品　*vt.* 装饰，美化
21. carpet ['kɑːpit] *n.* 地毯，地毯状覆盖物
22. fabric ['fæbrik] *n.* 织物，纸品；构造，结构
23. artichoke ['ɑːtitʃəuk] *n.* 洋蓟
24. inherent [in'hiərənt] *adj.* 固有的，内在的
25. rustic ['rʌstik] *adj.* 乡村的，质朴的
26. robust [rəu'bʌst] *adj.* 粗野的，粗鲁的
27. sculpture ['skʌlptʃə] *n.* 雕塑，雕刻，雕像
28. illustration [ˌiləs'treiʃən] *n.* 插图，图表；说明，图解，图示

29. decorative ['dekərətiv] *adj.* 装饰的，装饰性的
30. prelude ['prelju:d] *n.* 开端，序幕，前奏

Notes

〔1〕 the division of labor：劳动分工，在本文中是指工艺美术运动的理论家和艺术家认为机器化大生产带来了劳动分工，正是机器对手工的替代导致了产品外观的粗糙简陋，没有美的设计。

〔2〕 the Arts and Crafts style：工艺美术运动风格。该风格具有以下几个特点：（1）强调手工艺，明确反对机器化生产；（2）提倡哥特风格和其他中世纪风格；（3）主张设计的诚实、诚恳，讲究简单、朴实，反对华而不实的趋势；（4）装饰上推崇自然主义。

〔3〕 the Great Exhibition of 1851：1851年世界博览会，是1851年在英国伦敦的海德公园举行的全世界第一次博览会，主题内容是世界文化和工业科技。Great在此表示"伟大的、壮观的"。

〔4〕 Nikolaus Pevsner：尼古拉斯·佩夫斯纳（1902—1983），英国建筑历史学家，著有《建筑评论》、《现代设计的先驱》和《欧洲建筑概要》等著作。

〔5〕 Henry van de Velde：亨利·凡德·维尔德（1863—1957），比利时建筑师、设计教育家，德国新艺术运动领袖，德意志制造联盟创始人之一。

〔6〕 Art Nouveau：新艺术运动，是19世纪末20世纪初在欧洲和美国产生和发展的一次内容广泛的设计运动。

〔7〕 Vienna Secession：维也纳分离派（1897—1915），是在奥地利新艺术运动中产生的著名的艺术家组织，其代表人物有画家克里姆特、建筑家和设计师瓦格纳、霍夫曼等。

〔8〕 Bauhaus：包豪斯（1919—1933），是德国魏玛市公立包豪斯学校的简称，是世界上第一所完全为发展现代设计教育而建立的学校，对世界现代设计的发展产生了深远的影响。

Exercises

Choose the best answer to each question according to the text.

1. The Arts and Crafts Movement was an international design movement that originated in ____.
A. Germany
B. England
C. Vienna

2. The Arts and Crafts Movement was instigated by ____.
A. Henry van de Velde
B. Henry Cole and Owen Jones
C. William Morris and John Ruskin

3. The Arts and Crafts Movement was against the styles that had developed out of ____.
A. Art Nouveau
B. traditional craftsmanship
C. machine-production

4. William Morris thinks that a fabric or wallpaper might be decorated in _____.
A. a natural motif made to look as real as possible
B. an ornate and artificial motif
C. flowing curvilinear forms

Lesson 2 Art Nouveau

Art Nouveau is an international movement and style of art, architecture and applied art—especially the decorative arts—that peaked in popularity at the turn of the 20th century (1890–1905). The name 'Art Nouveau' is French for 'new art'. It is also known as Jugendstil, German for 'youth style', named after the magazine *Jugend* [1], which promoted it, and in Italy, Stile Liberty from the department store in London, Liberty & Co., which popularized the style[2]. As a reaction to the academic art of the 19th century, it is characterized by organic, especially floral and other plant-inspired motifs, as well as highly stylized and flowing curvilinear forms. Art Nouveau is an approach to design according to which artists should work on everything from architecture to furniture, making art part of everyday life. Typical products include the drawings of Beardsley[3], the furniture of Mackintosh[4], the architecture of Gaudi[5], the jewellery of Lalique[6], the glassware of Louis Comfort Tiffany[7], and the Paris Metro stations by Hector Guimard[8].

Aubrey Beardsley's illustration for Salome

Mira Apartment designed by Gaudi

Stained glass lamp designed by Tiffany

The Paris Metro station by Guimard

The movement was strongly influenced by Czech artist Alphonse Mucha[9], when Mucha produced a lithographed poster, which appeared on 1 January 1895 in the streets of Paris as an advertisement for the play *Gismonda* by Victorien Sardou, starring Sarah Bernhardt. It was an overnight sensation, and announced the new artistic style and its creator to the citizens of Paris. Initially called the Mucha Style, this soon became known as Art Nouveau.

Alphonse Mucha   Mucha's illustration for *Gismonda*

Dynamic, undulating, and flowing, with curved 'whiplash' lines of syncopated rhythm[10], characterised much of Art Nouveau. Another feature is the use of hyperbolas and parabolas. Conventional mouldings seem to spring to life and 'grow' into plant-derived forms[11]. As an art movement it has affinities with the Pre-Raphaelites and the Symbolism movement, and artists like Aubrey Beardsley, Alphonse Mucha, Edward Burne-Jones and Gustav Klimt could be classed in more than one of these styles. Unlike symbolist painting, however, Art Nouveau has a distinctive visual look; and unlike the backward-looking Arts and Crafts Movement, Art Nouveau artists quickly used new materials, machined surfaces, and abstraction in the service of pure design.

Japanese woodblock prints, with their curved lines, patterned surfaces, contrasting voids, and flatness of visual plane, also inspired Art Nouveau. Some line and curve patterns became graphic clichés that were later found in works of artists from all parts of the world.

Art Nouveau did not negate the machine as the Arts and Crafts Movement did, but used it to its advantages. For sculpture, the principal materials employed were glass and wrought iron, leading to sculptural qualities even in architecture.

Although Art Nouveau fell out of favour with the arrival of 20th-century modernist styles, it is seen today as an important bridge between the historicism of Neoclassicism and Modernism. Furthermore, Art Nouveau monuments are now recognized by UNESCO [12] on its World Heritage

List as significant contributions to cultural heritage. The historic center of Riga, Latvia, with 'the finest collection of art nouveau buildings in Europe', was inscribed on the list in 1997 in part because of the 'quality and the quantity of its Art Nouveau/Jugendstil architecture', and four Brussels town houses by Victor Horta were included in 2000 as 'works of human creative genius' that are 'outstanding examples of Art Nouveau architecture brilliantly illustrating the transition from the 19th to the 20th century in art, thought, and society'.

Background Information

Art Nouveau：新艺术。"新艺术"一词成为描绘兴起于19世纪末20世纪初的艺术运动及这一运动所产生的艺术风格的术语，它所涵盖的时间大约从1880年到1910年，跨度近30年，以比利时和法国为中心，用流畅性的自由曲线（特别以自然植物形状为基础）来造形，是在整个欧洲和美国展开的装饰艺术运动，在设计发展史上是由古典传统走向现代主义的一个必不可少的转折与过渡，其影响十分深远。

Words and Expressions

1. Art Nouveau ['nu:vəu] *n.* （法）新艺术，新艺术运动
2. applied [ə'plaid] *adj.* 应用的，实用的
3. peak [pi:k] *vi.* 达到高峰，达到最大值 *n.* 山峰，山顶；高峰，最高点
4. Jugendstil ['ju:gəntʃti:l] *n.* （德）新艺术（=Art Nouveau）
5. popularize ['pɔpjuləraiz] *vt.* 普及，使流行，使通俗化
6. reaction [ri'ækʃən] *n.* 反应，反对
7. academic [ˌækə'demik] *adj.* 学院的；学术的，理论的
8. organic [ɔ:'gænik] *adj.* 有机的，有机物的
9. floral ['flɔ:rəl] *adj.* 花的，似花的
10. motif [məu'ti:f] *n.* 装饰的图案或式样；主题，主旨
11. as well as 也，又；和……一样；不但……而且
12. flowing ['fləuiŋ] *adj.* 流动的，平滑的
13. curvilinear [ˌkə:vi'liniə] *adj.* 曲线的，由曲线而成的
14. approach [ə'prəutʃ] *n.* 靠近，接近；方法，方式
15. glassware ['glɑ:swɛə] *n.* 玻璃器皿，玻璃制品
16. Czech [tʃek] *adj.* 捷克的，捷克人的 *n.* 捷克人（语）
17. lithograph ['liθəgrɑ:f] *n.* 平版印刷
18. overnight sensation 一夜成名
19. dynamic [dai'næmik] *adj.* 力的，动力的；有活力的，有生气的
20. undulating ['ʌndjuleitiŋ] *adj.* 波状的，波状起伏的
21. whiplash ['wiplæʃ] *n.* 鞭打；鞭绳
22. syncopate ['siŋkəˌpeit] *vt.* （音乐的）切分
23. hyperbola [hai'pə:bələ] *n.* 双曲线
24. parabola [pə'ræbələ] *n.* 抛物线

25. moulding ['məuldiŋ] n. （墙壁、家具、画框等的）装饰线条；模具
26. affinity [ə'finiti] n. 姻亲；密切关系
27. symbolist ['simbəlist] n. 象征主义者，符号论者
28. distinctive [di'stiŋktiv] adj. 与众不同的，独特的
29. backward-looking ['bækwəd'lukiŋ] adj. 回顾过去的；保守的；退缩的
30. abstraction [æb'strækʃən] n. 抽象
31. woodblock ['wudblɔk] n. 木板，木块；木版，木刻画
32. void [vɔid] n. 空间；空隙；空虚
33. clichés [kli:'ʃeiz] （法）陈词滥调
34. negate [ni'geit] vt. 否认，否定；使无效
35. fall out of 从……掉了出来；失去
36. neoclassicism [,ni:əu'klæsə,sizəm] n. 新古典主义
37. heritage ['heritidʒ] n. 遗产，继承物
38. outstanding [,aut'stændiŋ] adj. 杰出的，优秀的，出色的

Notes

「1」新艺术这个名称没有被翻译成英语，因而在不同的国家有不同的名字。新艺术运动在德国是以"青年风格"来称谓的，它是以1896年德国艺术批评家朱利·梅耶·格拉佛创办的先锋派期刊《青年》杂志而得名的。

「2」在意大利，新艺术因为1875年阿瑟·拉塞卜·利伯蒂在伦敦开设的商店而得名"利伯特风格"。利伯蒂受东方进口丝绸的影响，创办了具有东方装饰风格的丝绸工厂，影响了当时新的装饰风格的产生。"Liberty"一词在英文里就是"自由"的意思，所以"自由风格"成为这种流行风格在意大利的代名词。

「3」Beardsley：奥勃利·比亚兹莱（Aubrey Beardsley，1872—1898），19世纪末英国著名的黑白插图装饰艺术家，以其平面装饰风格、清晰优美的线条和强烈的黑白色块而闻名于世。

「4」Mackintosh：麦金托什（1868—1928），苏格兰人，英国格拉斯哥（苏格兰首府）的建筑和产品设计师，代表作有格拉斯哥艺术学院和风山住宅等。

「5」Gaudi：安东尼奥·高迪（Antonio Gaudi，1852—1926），西班牙著名建筑师，代表作有米拉公寓、古埃尔公园、神圣家族教堂等，因其自然主义的建筑风格成为新艺术运动的代表。

「6」Lalique：瑞内·拉利克（René Lalique，1860—1945），法国著名珠宝和水晶设计师，是国际知名水晶品牌莱俪的创始人。

「7」Louis Comfort Tiffany：路易斯·康福特·蒂凡尼（1848—1933），美国艺术家，

以制造装饰性玻璃而闻名，他制造的灯和玻璃器皿外形流畅，颜色变幻无常，使蒂凡尼成为美国新艺术风格的主要倡导者。

［8］Hector Guimard：赫克多·吉马德（1867—1942），法国建筑设计师，代表作有巴黎地铁入口、贝朗榭公寓等。

［9］Alphonse Mucha：阿方斯·慕夏（1860—1939），捷克艺术家，他创作的海报是新艺术的典型代表。

［10］syncopate rhgthm：切分音，是旋律在进行当中，由于音乐的需要，音符的强拍和弱拍发生了变化而出现的节奏变化。

［11］plant-derived form：曲线装饰风格是新艺术运动的主要特征，这里是比喻曲线充满植物般的生命力。

［12］UNESCO：全称为United Nations Educational, Scientific and Cultural Organization，联合国教育、科学及文化组织，简称联合国教科文组织，属联合国专门机构。其宗旨是通过教育、科学和文化促进各国间合作，对和平和安全做出贡献。

Exercises

Read the following statements carefully, and decide whether they are true (T) or false (F) according to the text.

1. The name 'Art Nouveau' is German for 'youth style', named after the magazine *Jugend*.

2. The typical products of Art Nouveau include the drawings of Beardsley, the furniture of Mackintosh, the architecture of Gaudi, the wallpaper of William Morris, the glassware of Louis Comfort Tiffany, and the Paris Metro stations by Hector Guimard.

3. Art Nouveau was strongly influenced by Czech artist Alphonse Mucha and Japanese woodblock prints.

4. Art Nouveau negated the machine as the Arts and Crafts Movement did.

5. Art Nouveau is an important bridge between the historicism of Neoclassicism and Modernism.

Lesson 3   Constructivism

Russian Constructivism was a movement that was active from 1913 to the 1940s. It was a movement created by the Russian avant-garde, but quickly spread to the rest of the continent. Constructivist art is committed to completing abstraction with a devotion to modernity, where themes are often geometric, experimental and rarely emotional. Subjective or individualistic forms are far more suitable to the movement than objective forms carrying universal meanings. Constructivist themes are also quite minimal, where the artwork is broken down to its most basic elements. New media are often used in the creation of works, which helps to create a style of art that is orderly. An art of order was desirable at the time because it was just after WWI that the movement arose, which suggested a need for understanding, unity and peace. Famous artists of the Constructivist movement include Vladimir Tatlin[1], Kasimir Malevich[2], Alexander Rodchenko [3], and El Lissitzky[4].

Monument to the Third International, Vladimir Tatlin

Black Square, Kasimir Malevich

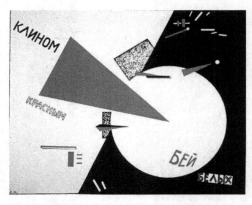
Poster '*Beat the Whites with the Red Wedge*', El Lissitzky

The artists of the movement were influenced by, and used materials from, industrial design such as sheet metal and glass. Often these materials were used to create geometrically-shaped objects, which were in keeping with the utilitarian artistic vision of the movement.

Tatlin's most famous piece remains his 'Monument to the Third International' (1919—1920, Moscow), a 22-ft-high iron frame on which rested a revolving cylinder, cube, and cone, all made of glass which was originally designed for massive scale. After the 1917 Revolution, Tatlin (considered the father of Russian Constructivism) worked for the new Soviet Education Commissariat which used artists and art to educate the public. During this period, he developed an officially authorized art form which utilized 'real materials in real space'. His project for a Monument of the Third International [5] marked his first foray into architecture and became a symbol for Russian avant-garde architecture and International Modernism.

Other painters, sculptors, and photographers working during this time were usually involved with industrial materials such as glass, steel, and plastic in clearly defined arrangements. Because of their admiration for machines and technology, functionalism, and modern media, the members were also called artist-engineers.

Background Information

Constructivism：构成主义，又名结构主义，是俄国十月革命胜利前后在俄国一小批先进知识分子当中产生的前卫艺术运动和设计运动。构成主义认为视觉艺术的某一要素，如线条、色彩、形式，都具有其自身的表现力，从而独立于世界表象的任何关系之外。构成主义对非客观形态、材料和机械结构的特质有着深入的思考和理解。

Words and Expressions

1. constructivism [kən'strʌktivizəm] *n.* 构成主义，构成派
2. active ['æktiv] *adj.* 活跃的，积极的；起作用的
3. avant-garde [ˌævɑːt'gɑːd] *n.* 革新者，（尤指）艺术上的先锋派 *adj.* 先锋的，前卫的
4. be commit to 致力于，献身
5. geometric [dʒiə'metrik] *adj.* 几何（学）的；几何图案的；成几何级数增加的
6. emotional [i'məuʃənl] *adj.* 感情的，情绪的；易动感情的，情绪激动的
7. individualistic [ˌindiˌvidjuə'listik] *adj.* 个人主义的
8. far more than 远远多于，不只
9. suitable ['suːtəbl] *adj.* 适合的，恰当的
10. minimal ['miniməl] *adj.* 最小的，极微的
11. orderly ['ɔːdəli] *adj.* 整齐的，有序的
12. desirable [di'zaiərəbl] *adj.* 值得向往的，值得拥有的；合适的，合意的，合乎要求的
13. sheet [ʃiːt] *adj.* 片状的
14. in keeping with 和……一致，与……协调
15. utilitarian [ˌjuːtili'tɛəriən] *adj.* 实用的；功利的；功利主义的
16. cylinder ['silində] *n.* 圆柱，圆筒，圆柱状物

17. cube [kju:b] *n.* 立方体，立方形物体；立方
18. cone [kəun] *n.* 圆锥体，锥形物
19. massive ['mæsiv] *adj.* 巨大的；大量的；大规模的
20. revolution [,revə'lu:ʃən] *n.* 革命，变革
21. authorize ['ɔ:θəraiz] *vt.* 批准，认可；授权，委托
22. foray ['fɔ:rei] *n.* 尝试；突袭
23. photographer [fə'tɔgrəfə] *n.* 摄影师
24. plastic ['plæstik] *n.* 塑料，塑料制品
25. defined [di'faind] *adj.* 定义明确的；清晰的；轮廓分明的
26. admiration [,ædmə'reiʃən] *n.* 钦佩，赞赏

Notes

「1」Vladimir Tatlin：弗拉基米尔·塔特林（1885—1953），俄国艺术家、雕塑家，构成主义运动的主要发起者，利用玻璃、金属、电线、木材等工业材料来进行抽象浮雕的创作，他1919—1920年完成的《第三国际纪念塔》是构成主义最重要的代表作。

「2」Kasimir Malevich：卡西米尔·马列维奇（1878—1935），俄国几何抽象画家，至上主义艺术奠基人。1913年，他在白纸上用铅笔画了一幅《黑方块》，这一简约新颖的构图成为至上主义产生的标志。

「3」Alexander Rodchenko：亚历山大·罗钦可（1891—1956），俄国著名摄影师，俄国构成主义的创始者之一。

「4」El Lissitzky：埃尔·李西茨基（1890—1956），俄国前卫艺术家，受到马列维奇的至上主义、塔特林的构成主义的影响，大约在1919年加入构成主义行列。1919年设计的海报《用红楔子攻打白色》是其著名的构成主义代表作。

「5」Monument of the Third International：第三国际纪念塔，十月革命后，塔特林担任了莫斯科苏维埃政府主管艺术工作的委员，后转入艺术文化研究所和艺术文化博物馆工作。1920年，塔特林受苏维埃政府的委托，设计了这座"第三国际纪念塔"。没有采用传统的建筑形式，而采用富有幻想性的现代雕塑形态。其中心体是由一个玻璃制成的核心、一个立方体、一个圆柱来合成的。这一晶亮的玻璃体好像比萨斜塔那样，倾悬于一个不对等的轴座上面，四周环绕着钢条做成的螺旋梯子。玻璃圆柱每年环绕轴座周转一次，里面的空间划分出教堂和会议室。玻璃核心则一个月周转一次，内部是各种活动的场所。

Exercises

Translate the following passage into Chinese.

Constructivism was an artistic and architectural movement that originated in Russia from 1919 onward which rejected the idea of 'art for arts sake' in favour of art as a practice directed towards social purposes. Constructivism as an active force lasted until around 1934, having a great deal of effect on developments in the art of the Weimar Republic and elsewhere, before being replaced by Socialist Realism. Its motifs have sporadically recurred in other art movements since.

Lesson 4 Bauhaus and the Education of Design

Des Staatliches Bauhaus[1], commonly known simply as Bauhaus, was a school in Germany that combined crafts and the fine arts, and was famous for the approach to design that it publicized and taught. It operated from 1919 to 1933. At that time the German term 'Bauhaus', literally 'house of construction' stood for the new building design system.

The Bauhaus school was founded by Walter Gropius in Weimar[2]. In spite of its name, and the fact that its founder was an architect, the Bauhaus did not have an architecture department during the first years of its existence. Nonetheless it was founded with the idea of creating a 'total' work of art[3] in which all arts, including architecture would eventually be brought together. The Bauhaus style became one of the most influential currents in Modernist architecture and modern design. The Bauhaus had a profound influence upon subsequent developments in art, architecture, graphic design, interior design, industrial design, and typography.

The school existed in three German cities (Weimar from 1919 to 1925, Dessau from 1925 to 1932 and Berlin from 1932 to 1933) [4], under three different presidents: Walter Gropius from 1919 to 1928, Hannes Meyer [5] from 1928 to 1930 and Ludwig Mies van der Rohe [6] from 1930 until 1933, when the school was closed by its own leadership under pressure from the Nazi regime.

Bauhaus building Walter Gropius

The Bauhaus curriculum combined theoretic education and practical vocational training in its educational workshops. As teachers, or Bauhaus masters, Gropius brought from all over Europe such men as Lyonel Feininger [7], Vassily Kandinsky [8], Paul Klee[9], Johannes Itten[10] and Laszlo Moholy-Nagy[11]. Marcel Breuer[12], Hannes Meyer and Josef Albers[13] also joined the faculty.

The educational process was as much responsible for innovation and new design paradigms as the philosophy of the Bauhaus. For example, Itten developed the innovative 'preliminary course' which was to teach students the basics of material characteristics, composition, and color. In 1920 he also published a book, *The Art of Color*, which describes these ideas as a furthering of Adolf Hölzel's [14] color wheel. Itten was one of the first people to define and identify strategies for successful color combinations. Through his research he devised seven methodologies for coordinating colors utilizing the hue's contrasting properties.

Beginning with a required preliminary course, students learned the basics of fine art (color theory, composition, drawing). After completing this requirement, the students then chose the discipline they wished to pursue, in specialized workshops for architecture, textile design, furniture design, typography, etc. This pedagogical system was soon copied by art and design schools all over the world. Students studied the problems of manufacturing, the requirements for housing large populations inexpensively, or bringing beauty as well as function into the home through fabric, furniture or utensils.

The Bauhaus school left its greatest impact in the field of applied design. Here, in designing for those objects of daily life which are mass-produced by industrial technology, it is perhaps harder to design a first-rate teapot than a second-rate painting. Modern design is now respected as a profession and an art. We are no longer surprised to see exhibits of modern furniture in museums such as the Museum of Modern Art[15] in New York.

   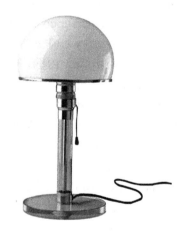

Wassily chair designed by Marcel Breuer   Lamps and lanterns designed by Wilhelm Wagenfeld Stiftung

Background Information

Bauhaus：包豪斯，是德国魏玛市"公立包豪斯学校"的简称，后改称"设计学院"，习惯上仍沿称"包豪斯"。包豪斯的创办者格罗佩斯把德文的"建筑"（bau）和"房子"（haus）两个词合一而创造了"Bauhaus"一词。包豪斯的成立标志着现代设计

的诞生，对世界现代设计的发展产生了深远的影响，也是世界上第一所完全为发展现代设计教育而建立的学院。

包豪斯的设计教育观念是：（1）技术和艺术应该和谐统一；（2）视觉敏感性达到理性的水平；（3）对材料、结构、肌理、色彩有科学的、技术的理解；（4）集体工作是设计的核心；（5）艺术家、企业家、技术人员应该紧密合作；（6）学生的作业和企业项目密切结合。

Words and Expressions

1. staatliches *adj.* （德）国家的，国有的，国立的
2. combine [kəm'bain] *vt.* 使联合，使结合
3. fine arts 美术，艺术
4. publicize ['pʌblisaiz] *vt.* 宣传，公布
5. operate ['ɔpəreit] *vt.* 工作，运转；经营，管理
6. literally ['litərəli] *adv.* 逐字地，照字面地
7. stand for 代表，象征，意味着；主张，支持
8. department [di'pɑ:tmənt] *n.* 部门，局，处，科，系
9. current ['kʌrənt] *n.* 水流，气流，电流；趋势，倾向，潮流
10. profound [prə'faund] *adj.* 深刻的，深度的，意义深远的
11. have an influence on/upon 对……有影响
12. subsequent ['sʌbsikwənt] *adj.* 后来的，随后的，继……之后的
13. interior [in'tiəriə] *adj.* 内的，内部的；国内的，内地的
14. interior design 室内设计
15. typography [tai'pɔgrəfi] *n.* 印刷术，印刷工艺，排版
16. Nazi ['nɑ:tsi] *n.* 纳粹党，法西斯分子
17. regime [rei'ʒi:m] *n.* 政权，政体，统治（方式）
18. curriculum [kə'rikjuləm] *n.* 课程，全部课程
19. workshop ['wə:kʃɔp] *n.* 工场，车间；研讨会，讲习班
20. faculty ['fækəlti] *n.* （大学或院、系的）全体教职员，（从事某一专门职业的）全体人员
21. be responsible for 对……负责，对……有责任
22. paradigm ['pærə,daim] *n.* 范例，典范
23. preliminary [pri'liminəri] *adj.* 初步的，预备的，开端的
24. composition [,kɔmpə'ziʃən] *n.* 构成，构图
25. color wheel 色彩环（=color circle）
26. strategy ['strætidʒi] *n.* 策略，计谋

27. methodology [ˌmeθə'dɔlədʒi] *n.* 方法学，方法论
28. coordinate [kəu'ɔ:dineit] *vt.* 使协调，使一致
29. utilize ['ju:tilaiz] *vt.* 利用，使用
30. hue [hju:] *n.* 色彩，色调，色相
31. discipline ['disiplin] *n.* 学科
32. pedagogical [ˌpedə'gɔdʒikl] *adj.* 教学（法）的
33. fabric ['fæbrik] *n.* 织物；结构，构造
34. utensil [ju:'tensl] *n.* 器皿，用具
35. mass-produced [ˌmæs prə'dju:st] *adj.* 大批量生产的
36. first-rate [ˌfə:st'reit] *adj.* 第一流的，最佳的；最高级的
37. teapot ['ti:pɔt] *n.* 茶壶

Notes

［1］Des Staatliches Bauhaus：德语，意为"国立包豪斯"。

［2］Weimar：魏玛，德国城市名，拥有众多文化古迹，曾是德国的文化中心。

［3］'total' work of art：包豪斯的教员康定斯基1911年撰写的《关于艺术的精神》一书认为，未来的艺术一定是多种媒介的综合，不会再是单一媒体的表现。康定斯基称之为Gesamtkunstwerk过程，这个德文词被翻译成英语的'total' work of art，即艺术创作的综合。这个术语并非康定斯基创造的，它其实是德国音乐家瓦格纳最早开始使用的，康定斯基把它首先用于视觉艺术的创作与教育上，并得到格罗佩斯的认同。

［4］魏玛、德绍和柏林构成了包豪斯学校的三个阶段：该校在1919年创立于魏玛，因政治原因于1925年迁至德绍，1932年又被赶出德绍，勉强在柏林栖身，1933年纳粹上台更是被勒令解散。

［5］Hannes Meyer：汉斯•迈耶（1889—1954），瑞士建筑师，包豪斯第二任校长。

［6］Ludwig Mies van der Rohe：路德维希•密斯•凡德罗（1886—1969），德国建筑师，也是著名的现代主义建筑大师，包豪斯的第三任校长。

［7］Lyonel Feininger：利奥尼•费宁格（1871—1956），著名的表现主义画家，1919—1933年在包豪斯担任形式导师。

［8］Vassily Kandinsky：瓦西里•康定斯基（1866—1944），俄国画家和美术理论家，现代抽象艺术理论和实践的奠基人。康定斯基对包豪斯基础课程的贡献主要在于两个方面：分析绘画和对色彩与形体的理论研究。

［9］Paul Klee：保罗•克利（1879—1940），德国画家，生于瑞士，表现主义大师，1920—1931年在包豪斯任教。

［10］Johannes Itten：约翰内斯•伊顿（1888—1967），瑞士人，著名的美术理论家和艺术教育家，毕生从事色彩学的研究，包豪斯早期教员、基础课程的创造者之一。

［11］Laszlo Moholy-Nagy：拉兹洛•莫霍利•纳吉（1895—1946），匈牙利人，艺术家和理论家，1937年移居美国，把包豪斯的理论和教学观念带到了美国，在芝加哥创办了一个"新包豪斯"，这就是以后的芝加哥设计学院。

「12」Marcel Breuer：马歇·布劳耶（1902—1981），匈牙利人，包豪斯的第一期学生，毕业后任包豪斯家具部门的教师，主持家具车间。

「13」Josef Albers：约瑟夫·亚伯斯（1888—1976），德国画家、设计师，极简主义大师，1923—1933年在包豪斯任教。

「14」Adolf Hölzel：阿道夫·霍尔茨尔（1853—1934），德国印象派画家。

「15」the Museum of Modern Art：纽约现代艺术博物馆，简称MOMA，坐落在纽约市曼哈顿城中，位于曼哈顿第53街（在第五和第六大道之间），是当今世界最重要的现当代美术博物馆之一，与英国伦敦泰特美术馆、法国蓬皮杜国家文化和艺术中心等齐名。

Exercises

Read the following statements carefully, and decide whether they are true (T) or false (F) according to the text.

1. The Bauhaus has an architecture department during the first years of its existence.
2. The Bauhaus curriculum paid more attention to theoretic education than practical vocational training.
3. The innovative 'preliminary course' which was to teach students the basics of material characteristics, composition, and color was developed by Itten.
4. Before completing a required preliminary course, the students chose the discipline they wished to pursue.
5. The Bauhaus pedagogical system was adopted by art and design schools all over the world.
6. The Bauhaus school left its greatest impact in the field of fine arts.

Lesson 5 The International Typographic Style

Also known as the Swiss Style, the International Typographic Style is a graphic design style developed in Switzerland in the 1950s that emphasizes cleanliness, readability and objectivity. It was an extension of Bauhaus principles developed mainly in Zürich and Basle[1] in the period leading up to the Second World War. Key figures in the evolution of the Style included Theo Ballmer[2], Max Billr[3], and Max Huber[4], all of whom were familiar with the avant-garde ideals of De Stijl[5], Constructivism, and *The New Typography* [6] of the interwar years.

The rational characteristics of the Style were its use of sans serif typography (especially the Helvetica and Univers typefaces[7]), text set in narrow columns with a rigid left-hand margin and unjustified right. This austere, geometrically conceived, and rational outlook was further defined by its use of photography rather than hand-drawn illustrations. Swiss neutrality during the war had allowed these design principles to develop uninterrupted and it was increasingly adopted in design-conscious circles internationally in the 1950s, 1960s, and 1970s.

Helvetica   Publication from the Hochschule für Gestaltung Ulm

Its influence was widely disseminated through the Swiss-based journal *New Graphic Design* (1958—1965), edited by Josef Müller-Brockmann[8], Hans Neuburg[9], and Richarde Lohse[10], and its layout was consonant with the design principles that its contributors espoused, a visual embodiment of the corporate aesthetic of many multinationals in the United States. This came under attack from a new generation of typographers identified with New Wave Design[11] who sought to counter the rigidity of the Swiss Style with a more expressive, intuitive style linked to the tenets of Postmodernism.

New Graphic Design (magazine) published in 1958—1965   Poster designed by Josef Müller-Brockmann

Background Information

the International Typographic Style：国际主义平面设计风格。20世纪50年代期间，一种崭新的平面设计风格终于在联邦德国与瑞士形成，被称为"瑞士平面设计风格"。20世纪50年代形成的国际主义风格的核心部分是无饰线字体的发展及广泛采用。新一代的平面设计家采用一种直截了当的新无饰线字体，达到高度的、毫无掩饰的视觉传达目的。由于这种风格简单明确，传达功能准确，因此很快流行于全世界，成为二战后影响最大、国际上最流行的设计风格，因此又被称为国际主义平面设计风格。

Words and Expressions

1. Switzerland ['switsələnd] *n.* 瑞士
2. readability [,ri:də'biləti] *n.* 易读，可读性
3. interwar ['intəwɔ:] *adj.* 两次战争之间的
4. sans [sænz] *prep.* 无
5. serif ['serif] *n.* （印）截线，衬线
6. column ['kɔləm] *n.* （报纸、杂志的）栏，段
7. rigid ['ridʒid] *adj.* 精确的，严密的
8. margin ['mɑ:dʒin] *n.* 页面空白
9. unjustified [ʌn'dʒʌstifaid] *adj.* 不正当的
10. austere [ɔ:'stiə] *adj.* 朴素的，无装饰的
11. neutrality [nju:'træləti] *n.* 中立，中立地位
12. uninterrupted ['ʌn,intə'rʌptid] *adj.* 不间断的，连续的
13. disseminate [di'semineit] *vt.* 散播，传播

14. consonant ['kɔnsənənt] *adj.* 符合的，一致的
15. espouse [is'pauz] *vt.* 拥护，支持
16. embodiment [im'bɔdimənt] *n.* 体现，具体化
17. multinational [ˌmʌlti'næʃənl] *adj.* 多国的，跨国公司的
18. rigidity [ri'dʒidəti] *n.* 死板，刻板
19. expressive [iks'presiv] *adj.* 有表现力的，情感丰富的
20. intuitive [in'tju:itiv] *adj.* 直觉的，直观的
21. tenet ['tenit] *n.* 宗旨，原则
22. postmodernism [ˌpəust'mɔdənizəm] *n.* 后现代主义

Notes

「1」Zürich and Basle：苏黎世和巴塞尔，分别为瑞士的第一大和第三大城市。作为第二次世界大战前后最重要的平面设计中心之一，这两个城市对国际主义风格的形成起到重要作用，成为一个设计中心地区，涌现出了艾米尔·路德（1914—1970）、阿明·霍夫曼（1920—2020）等重要的平面设计师。

「2」Theo Ballmer：西奥·巴尔莫（1902—1965），瑞士平面设计家，毕业于包豪斯学校，是最早采用完全的、绝对的数学方式从事平面设计构造的设计家之一。

「3」Max Billr：马克斯·比尔（1908—1994），瑞士设计师，毕业于包豪斯学校，主要从事建筑设计，1950—1955年期间任联邦德国乌尔姆设计学院第一任院长。

「4」Max Huber：马克斯·胡珀（1912—1992），瑞士平面设计家。

「5」De Stijl：荷兰风格派，又称新造型主义（neoplasticism），1917—1928年由蒙德里安等人在荷兰创立。其绘画宗旨是完全拒绝使用任何的具象元素，只用单纯的色彩和几何形象来表现纯粹的精神。

「6」*The New Typography*：《新版面设计》，是德国设计师简·奇措德（Jan Tschichold）于1928年出版的著作，主张采用新的平面设计风格，认为越简单的版面越达到准确和有效的视觉传达效果。

「7」the Helvetica and Univers typefaces：字体的名称。Helvetica是赫尔维提加体，是由爱德华·霍夫曼和马克斯·梅丁格设计的，这种字体设计得非常完美，因此成为20世纪50年代到70年代最流行的字体，直到现在仍是流行的无衬线体。Univers是通用体，是瑞士平面设计家阿德里安·弗鲁提格创造的新无衬线体。

「8」Josef Müller-Brockmann：约塞夫·穆勒-布鲁克曼，瑞士平面设计师和设计教育家，主张设计以传达功能优秀为最高目的的宗旨。

「9」Hans Neuburg：汉斯·纽伯格，瑞士国际主义平面设计风格设计师之一。

「10」Richarde Lohse：理查德·洛斯（1902—1988），生于瑞士苏黎世，著名平面设计艺术家。

「11」New Wave Design：新浪潮平面设计运动。20世纪六七十年代的设计家开始感到瑞士发展起来的国际主义平面设计风格的刻板性必须进行改革，才能适合新时代的审美需求，因此对字体、编排的纵横粗细方式进行了形式主义的加工，增加了平面的趣味性和

韵味，不再是单调、刻板、高度理性的国际主义风格，而是充满了趣味、个人特色的新设计风格。

Exercises

Translate the following passage into Chinese.

The hallmarks of the International Typographic Style were: the use of a mathematical grid to provide an overall orderly and unified structure; sans serif typefaces (especially Helvetica, introduced in 1961) in a flush left and ragged right format; and black and white photography in place of drawn illustration. The overall impression is simple and rational, tightly structured and serious, clear and objective, and harmonious.

Unit Two

The Special Topics About Design

Lesson 6 Corporate Identity

All new business owners know the importance of corporate identity. Though there are a number of companies and service providers who achieve success without any corporate identity development strategy, most in time will realize that corporate identity is needed to continue on to the next level of success. If a company decides not to venture toward corporate development, they will run the risk of losing any existing consumer loyalty and could become dangerously stagnant.

In most cases, planning of your corporate identity starts with an exploratory and experimental phase. During this phase companies can work to review previous strategic materials as well as conduct precious consumer research testing. Some companies will also complete thorough management interviews to gain perspective on what others feel the company stands for and symbolizes to potential consumers.

Once all of the information from this initial discovery phase is collected, companies can then move on to corporate identity development and definition process. To complete this secondary phase successfully, some companies choose to bring together a branding team which, in addition to finalizing any needed corporate identity ,will also work to build company morale.

In marketing, a corporate identity is the 'persona' of a corporation which is designed to accord with and facilitate the attainment of business objectives. It is usually visibly manifested by the way of branding and the use of trademarks.

Corporate identity comes into being when there is a common ownership of an organizational philosophy that is manifested in a distinct corporate culture — the corporate personality. At its most profound, the public feel that they have ownership of the philosophy. Often referred to as organizational identity, corporate identity helps organizations to answer questions like 'Who are we?' and 'Where are we going?' Corporate identity also allows consumers to denote their sense of belonging with particular human aggregates or groups.

In general, this amounts to a corporate title, logo, logotype, color, and supporting devices commonly assembled within a set of guidelines. These guidelines govern how the identity is applied and confirm approved colour palettes, typefaces, page layouts and other such methods of maintaining visual continuity and brand recognition across all physical manifestations of the brand. These guidelines are usually formulated into a package of tools called corporate identity manuals.

Many companies, such as McDonald's and Electronic Arts [1], have their own identity that runs through all of their products and merchandise. The trademark 'M' logo and the yellow and red appears consistently throughout McDonald's packaging and advertisements. Many companies pay large amounts of money for the research, design and execution involved in creating an identity that is extremely distinguishable and appealing to the company's target audience.

McDonald's Logo   Electronic Arts's Logo

Corporate identity is often viewed as being composed of three parts:

Corporate design (logos, logotype, corporate colours, etc.)

Corporate communication (advertising, public relations, information, etc.)

Corporate behavior (internal values, norms, etc.)

Corporate identity has become a universal technique for promoting companies and improving corporate culture. Most notable is the CoCoMAS committee [2] and the company PAOS [3], both founded by Motoo Nakanishi [4] in Tokyo, Japan in 1968. Nakanishi fused design, management consulting and corporate culture to revolutionize corporate identity in Japan. In the United States, graphic design firms such as Chermayeff & Geismar [5] pioneered the application of modernist principles to corporate identity design.

Motoo Nakanishi   Chermayeff & Geismar

Corporate identity can seem like a challenging task, but the truth is by thinking creatively, listening to their consumers even the smallest of companies can achieve corporate identity victory!

Background Information

corporate identity：企业形象（企业形象设计），简称CI设计，是针对企业经营理念与精神文化，整体传达给企业内部与社会大众，并使其对企业产生一致的认同感或价值观，从而形成良好的企业形象和促销产品的设计系统。企业形象是企业自身的一项重要的无形资产，因为它代表着企业的信誉、产品质量、人员素质等。塑造企业形象虽然不一定能马上给企业带来经济效益，但它能创造良好的社会效益，获得社会认同感，最终会获得由社会效益转化来的经济效益。因此，塑造企业形象便成为具有长远眼光的企业的长期战略。

Words and Expressions

1. identity [ai'dentiti] n. 个性，特征
2. corporate identity 企业形象
3. run the risk of 冒险，冒……风险
4. stagnant ['stægnənt] adj. 停滞不前的
5. exploratory [iks'plɔ:rətəri] adj. 探索的
6. precious ['preʃəs] adj. 宝贵的，珍贵的
7. perspective [pə'spektiv] n. 看法，观点
8. brand [brænd] n. 品牌，商标
9. morale [mə'ra:l] n. 士气，斗志
10. persona [pə:'səunə] n. 人格面貌，外表形象
11. facilitate [fə'siliteit] vt. 促进，帮助
12. trademark ['treidma:k] n. 商标
13. refer to as 作为，把……当作
14. denote [di'nəut] vt. 表示，指示
15. aggregate ['ægrigeit] n. 集聚，凝聚 vt. 使聚集
16. amount to 相当于，意味着；合计，总数达到
17. logotype ['lɔgətaip] n. 标准字体
18. assemble [ə'sembl] vt. 集合，聚集
19. approved [ə'pru:vd] adj. 被认可的
20. palette ['pælit] n. 调色板
21. continuity [,kɔnti'nju:iti] n. 连续性，连贯性
22. formulate ['fɔ:mjuleit] vt. 规划，构想
23. manual ['mænjuəl] n. 手册，指南

24. distinguishable [dis'tiŋgwiʃəbl] *adj.* 可区别的，可辨别的
25. target ['tɑ:git] *n.* 目标

Notes

「1」Electronic Arts：美国艺电公司，简称EA，是全球著名的互动娱乐软件公司，创建于1982年，主要经营各种电子游戏的开发、出版及销售业务。

「2」CoCoMAS committee：企业经营战略传播委员会，CoCoMAS的全称为Corporate Communication as a Management Strategy，是中西元男在PAOS公司的经营理念中，为倡导建立"企业的文化与文化的存在企业"的理想而设置的研究委员会，以不断地研究开发经营上新的观念及思想。

「3」PAOS：全称为Progressive Artists Open System，著名的咨询顾问机构，为国际上一百多家跨国企业进行过各类咨询顾问服务。

「4」Motoo Nakanishi：中西元男，日本企业形象之父，全球最负盛名的企业经营策划大师、PAOS流CI创始人，日本CI战略会议最高顾问。中西元男为世界500强企业中的100强企业做过资源经营整合，如尼桑、马自达、大荣百货、石桥轮胎、麒麟啤酒、日本电信、住友银行、健伍、每日新闻、松屋百货等企业。

「5」Chermayeff & Geismar：谢苗耶夫和盖斯马设计公司，美国著名的品牌设计公司，由伊万·谢苗耶夫和汤姆·盖斯马创办，曾为美孚石油、美国公共广播公司（PBS）、大通银行、施乐、美国国家地理杂志等设计形象。

Exercises

Topics for oral discussion.

1. What do you think about the concept that a corporate identity is the 'persona' of a corporation which is usually visibly manifested by the way of branding and the use of trademarks?

2. Talk about your view on the classic cases of corporate identity design.

Lesson 7 Book Designer Fiona Raven

Book designer Fiona Raven offers worry-free book design for authors worldwide, including book cover design and interior page design. The following article comes from her personal website.

Participate in every stage of your book design for a creative, rewarding experience. Together we'll transform your ideas into a top-quality book you'll be proud of. I'll help you avoid costly pitfalls in production and make sure your book gets to press on time and on budget. I love books and am committed to making your book the best it can be.

Book design: an author's next step

You've worked hard to finish your manuscript, and you're ready for the next step: to transform it into a finished book. But where do you start?—you're a writer, not a designer. You've never shopped for a designer before, and you're a bit overwhelmed by the task. What happens if you're not satisfied with how your book turned out? And, if you don't know much about book production, how will you know whether things are on track?

Enjoying the process

Take the worry and stress out of book design by placing your book in the hands of someone you can trust. I know how to make your book the best it can be. You'll enjoy the creative process of participating in your book's design and seeing it evolve, and you can leave all the production details to me with complete confidence.

130+ successful book projects

I've designed more than 130 books for authors and publishers, including novels, children's books, nonfiction books and coffee table books [1]. My clients come from all walks of life. Most are first-time authors. Some are repeat clients with their second or third book; others are well-established publishers.

A top-quality book you'll love

What do ALL my clients have in common? They've each received a top-quality, professionally designed book that they love, as well as my prompt personal attention throughout the production of their book. So will you. You can relax knowing that you'll be guided through every stage of your book design from start to finish.

What my clients say:

'Best product possible.'

As a first-time author, it was a pleasure working with Fiona. She guided me through the development steps and brought up issues that I would have never anticipated on my own. She also provided me with contacts in proofreading, indexing and printing. She is extremely detail-oriented and wants to develop the best product possible. Her knowledge, professionalism and patience made the design process easy and enjoyable, as she brought our vision to fruition. We would like to do a second edition of our book, and would not think of working with anyone else!

—GERALD BLAKEY, PHARM.D., co-author of *Conquering the Cough & Cold Aisle Redondo Beach*, CA, USA

'None compare to level of service and quality of product.'

In addition to Fiona's top-notch design abilities, her professionalism from the beginning to the end of our project provided much confidence that all the bases were being covered. I've been through this process before with other designers but none compare to the level of service and quality of product that we got from Fiona.

—MARY McCOY, VP [2] of Training Group of the Pacific, publisher of *Making Sense of Tonga*, Nuku'alofa [3], Tonga

'Level of trust is priceless.'

Working with Fiona on my second edition was so much better than the experience I'd had getting my first edition produced with a different service! Fiona was easy to reach, there were no significant delays, and she was always there for me. Plus, I never felt like I was bothering her when I asked for changes. In fact, Fiona was consistently so calm and reassuring, I always feel more relaxed after talking with her than before. To a nervous author handing their work over to someone else, that level of trust is priceless!

—TANYA HARTER PIERCE, author of *Outsmart Your Cancer: Alternative Non-Toxic Treatments That Work*, State Line, NV, USA

Satisfaction guaranteed

And if we do work together on your book, I'm confident that you'll be completely satisfied with both the quality of your book and the level of service I provide. In fact, I guarantee it.

Request a quote for your book

Visit my Request a Quote page, then call or e-mail me to discuss your book—at no charge. If you like I can give you a firm quote after our discussion.

Remember, the road to publishing your book doesn't have to be full of potholes! It can be creative, rewarding and trouble-free all the way.

Background Information

Fiona Raven：加拿大书籍设计师，毕业于加拿大艾米利卡尔艺术与设计学院视觉艺术专业。

Words and Expressions

1. worry-free ['wʌri,fri:] *adj.* 无忧的，无需担心的
2. participate [pɑ:'tisipeit] *vi.* 参加，参与
3. stage [steidʒ] *n.* 阶段，时期
4. rewarding [ri'wɔ:diŋ] *adj.* 有益的；有报酬的；值得的
5. be proud of 以……自豪，对……感到满意
6. pitfall ['pitfɔ:l] *n.* 陷阱，圈套
7. on budget 在预算内（的）
8. manuscript ['mænjuskript] *n.* 手稿，原稿
9. overwhelm [,əuvə'welm] *vt.* 使不安，使不知所措；压倒，征服
10. on track 走上正轨
11. evolve [i'vɔlv] *vt.& vi.* 逐步形成；发展，进化
12. detail ['di:teil] *n.* 细节，详情
13. confidence ['kɔnfidəns] *n.* 信任，信赖；自信，信心
14. nonfiction [,nɔn'fikʃən] *n.* 非小说类文学作品
15. all walks of life 各行各业
16. well-established ['weli'stæbliʃt] *adj.* 固定下来的，已为大家所接受的，根深蒂固的
17. prompt [prɔmpt] *adj.* 及时的，迅速的
18. bring up 提出
19. issue ['iʃu:, 'isju:] *n.* 问题；争论，争议
20. anticipate [æn'tisipeit] *vt.* 预料；预期，期望
21. proofread ['pru:f,ri:d] *vt.* 校对
22. index ['indeks] *n.* 索引；卡片索引；文献索引
23. Pharm.D. （医）药学博士（Pharmaciae Doctor的缩写）
24. compare to 与……相比
25. top-notch [tɔp'nɔtʃ] *adj.* 拔尖的，出众的
26. make sense of 理解，了解
27. significant [sig'nifikənt] *adj.* 重要的，重大的
28. plus [plʌs] *prep.* 外加，另有
29. bother ['bɔðə] *vt.* 打搅，烦扰，打扰
30. reassuring [,ri:ə'ʃuəriŋ] *adj.* 安慰的；鼓气的；可靠的
31. outsmart [aut'smɑ:t] *vt.* 比……更聪明，智胜
32. alternative [ɔ:l'tə:nətiv] *adj.* 替代的；供选择的
33. non-toxic [nɔn 'tɔksik] *adj.* 无毒的
34. guaranteed [gærən'ti:d] *adj.* 必定的，肯定的
35. quote [kwəut] *n.* 报价

36. no charge 免收费用

37. pothole ['pɔthəul] *n.* 窝穴；道路上的坑洞

Notes

「1」coffee table books：咖啡桌上的摆设书籍，多为装帧精美、图文并茂的大开本画册。

「2」VP：副总裁，为企业职位的英文缩写，全称为vice president。

「3」Nuku'alofa：努库阿洛法，是汤加王国政府、王室所在地，也是汤加的工商业中心、交通枢纽和进出口货物集散地。

Exercises

Translate the following passage into Chinese.

The front cover is the front of the book, and usually contains at least the title and author, with possibly an appropriate illustration, in order to identify it as such. On the inside of the cover page, extending to the facing page is the front endpaper sometimes referred as FEP. The free half of the end paper is called a flyleaf. Traditionally, in hand-bound books, the endpaper is just a sheet of blank or ornamented paper physically masking and reinforcing the connection between the cover and the body of the book. In modern books it can be either plain, as in many text-oriented books, or richly ornamented and illustrated in more daringly designed editions as children books, coffee table books, etc.

The spine is the vertical edge of a book as it normally stands on a bookshelf. It is customary for it to have printed text on it. In texts published and/or printed in the United States, the spine text, when vertical, runs from the top to the bottom, such that it is right side up when the book is lying flat with the front cover on top. In books of Europe, the vertical spine text traditionally runs from the bottom up, though this convention has been changing lately. The spine usually contains all, or some, of four elements, and in the following order: (1) author, editor, or compiler; (2) title; (3) publisher; and (4) publisher logo.

On the inside of the back cover page, extending from the facing page before it, is the endpaper. Its design matches the front endpaper and, in accordance with it, contains either plain paper or pattern, image, etc. The back cover often contains biographical matter about the author or editor, and quotes from other sources praising the book. It may also contain a summary or description of the book.

Lesson 8 Successful Industrial Design

Industrial design is a combination of applied art and applied science, whereby the aesthetics, ergonomics[1] and usability of products may be improved for marketability and production. Industrial designers use the disciplines of art, business, and engineering to design everyday products—from smart phones to medical equipment to household goods. Each day, you rely on products designed by industrial designers. It is these designers who are responsible for a manufactured products' style, function (or usability), quality, and safety.

The term 'industrial design' is often attributed to the designer Joseph Claude Sinel[2] (although he himself denied it in later interviews) but the discipline predates that by at least a decade. Its origins lay in the industrialization of consumer products. For instance, the Deutscher Werkbund[3], founded in 1907 and a precursor to the Bauhaus, was a state-sponsored effort to integrate traditional crafts and industrial mass-production techniques, to put Germany on a competitive footing with England and the United States.

Industrial design also has a focus on technical concepts, products and processes. In addition to considering aesthetics, usability, and ergonomics, it can also encompass the engineering of objects, usefulness, market placement, and other concerns such as seduction, psychology, desire, and the emotional attachment of the user to the object.

Developing a product can seem like a daunting task but if you know the basic steps and phases required things will be much easier. Successful industrial design can be broken into 7 steps.

Problem assessment

It is a good idea to write down what the problem is first. Don't write down the solution to the problem at this point, even if you know how to do so. You simply need to state what the problem is and nothing more. I have seen the development of new products become complicated and time-consuming simply because the problem was never written down. A proper statement of the problem helps keep everyone on the same page and works to eliminate project creep.

Design specification

This is the step in which a solution to the previously defined problem begins to form. At this point a list of requirements of everything you can think of should be written down. You are not coming up with a solution just yet only setting the requirements necessary to create the product. Some examples of what should be on your list include, a retail price (how much people are willing to pay for this), size of the object (whether it needs to fit into someone's hand or through a door or in a garage), how fast it should go, whether it needs to be waterproof, what it should be made of, whether it uses batteries or plug into the wall. This list can go on and on but the important thing is that you list what is important to you. This list will help you and your designer in the next step.

Idea generation

Now you are getting somewhere, the problem has been defined and requirements have been set. At this point you should brainstorm[4] and sketch out your ideas. Don't worry if the drawings are not pretty, you are only trying to see if the concepts could work or if there is an obvious flaw. If you are not mechanically inclined, you may want to find someone who specializes in product or industrial design to help. Many design companies have no problem meeting with you to discuss and sketch a few ideas before you will be under any obligation to sign a contract or pay anything. You will want to come up with one or two good ideas before moving to the next step.

Concept design

Once at least one good idea for the new product has been sketched, you will want to have the design worked out in a little more detail. The designer will come up with a basic 3D design on a computer that is detailed enough to be sure the idea will work but not so detailed that it takes more than just a few hours to complete. This is the last step where an idea is either given the green light or trashed.

Detailed design

Now that a solid concept design has been created, it's time to get down to the details. In this phase the designer will create full detail 3D virtual models of all parts, work out design problems, create assembly and part drawings for every part, find suppliers for all purchased components and create 3D physical prototypes if necessary. This phase is complete when all problems have been solved and a full set of drawings have been delivered.

Testing

Testing is a very important part of product design and should not be overlooked. This step can be as simple as having a few people use the product for feedback or as complicated as sending it to a testing laboratory such as UL[5] for a thorough testing by professionals. The level of testing will most likely be determined by requirements of any retail stores that will be selling the product. It is important that you have someone test the product that has not been involved in the design process even if it's a friend. Someone who has not been part of the design will give a less biased opinion plus you can watch for any difficulty they may have using the product.

Manufacturing

The final step in the design process is manufacturing. In this step you or your designer will find suitable manufacturing facilities to create the product. You will need to come up with an agreement with the manufacturer on the terms of what they will be providing, the cost and when it will be delivered.

iPod Touch designed by Jonathan Ive[6] 　　Lemon juicer designed by Phillipe Starck[7]

Background Information

industrial design：工业设计，在我国早期也被翻译为"产品设计"，近年来统一称为"工业设计"。广义的概念是指以工学、美学、经济学为基础对工业产品进行设计，为20世纪初工业化社会的产物。狭义的工业设计指的是产品设计（product design），通过对人类生理、心理、生活习惯等一切关于人的自然属性和社会属性的认知，结合材料、技术、结构、工艺、形态、色彩、成本等因素，进行产品功能、性能、形式、价格、使用环境的定位的创意设计。本文中指的是狭义的工业设计范畴。

Words and Expressions

1. whereby [hwɛə'bai] conj. 凭借
2. aesthetic [i:s'θetik] adj. 美学的，审美的
3. ergonomics [ˌə:gə'nɔmiks] n. 人机工程学，工效学
4. usability [ˌju:zə'biliti] n. 可用性
5. marketability [ˌmɑ:kitə'biliti] n. 有销路，畅销
6. smart [smɑ:t] adj. 聪明的，伶俐的
7. attribute [ə'tribju:t] vt. 把……归因于，把……归咎于
8. predate [pri:'deit] vt. 在日期上早于，居先
9. lie in 在于
10. precursor [pri'kə:sə] n. 先驱，先锋，前身
11. integrate ['intigreit] vt. 使成一体，使结合，使合并
12. footing ['futiŋ] n. 地位；基础；立足点

13. encompass [in'kʌmpəs] *vt.* 包含，包括
14. seduction [si'dʌkʃən] *n.* 诱惑，引诱
15. daunting ['dɔ:ntiŋ] *adj.* 使人畏缩的
16. assessment [ə'sesmənt] *n.* 评价，评估；估价
17. at this point 此时，在这个时候
18. complicate ['kɔmpli,keit] *vt.* 使复杂，使错综
19. on the same page 意见一致
20. creep [kri:p] *vi.* 缓慢地行进，蹑手蹑脚地走
21. specification [,spesifi'keiʃən] *n.* 详述，说明
22. come up with 提出，提供
23. retail ['ri:teil] *n.* 零售
24. battery ['bætəri] *n.* 电池，蓄电池
25. plug [plʌg] *n.* 插头，插座
26. brainstorm ['brein,stɔ:m] *n.* 集思广益，集体研讨
27. sketch out 草拟；概述
28. flaw [flɔ:] *n.* 缺陷，缺点
29. trash [træʃ] *vt.* 丢弃，把……视为废物
30. solid ['sɔlid] *adj.* （俚）好的，满意的
31. get down to 开始认真处理，着手做
32. virtual ['və:tjuəl] *adj.* 虚拟的
33. assembly [ə'sembli] *n.* 装配，组装
34. overlook [,əuvə'luk] *vt.* 忽略，忽视
35. feedback ['fi:dbæk] *n.* 反应，反馈
36. biased ['baiəst] *adj.* 有偏见的，片面的

Notes

「1」ergonomics：人机工程学、工效学。人机工程学是一门多学科的交叉学科，研究的核心问题是不同的作业中人、机器及环境三者间的协调，研究方法和评价手段涉及心理学、生理学、医学、人体测量学、美学和工程技术多个领域，研究的目的则是通过各学科知识的应用，指导工作器具、工作方式和工作环境的设计和改造，使得作业在效率、安全、健康、舒适等几个方面的特性得以提高。

「2」Joseph Claude Sinel：约瑟夫·克劳德·西奈尔（1889—1975），美国设计师。1919年，西奈尔开设了自己的设计事务所，在事务所的信封上第一次使用了"工业设计"这个词。

「3」Deutscher Werkbund：德意志制造联盟，是1907年成立的一个积极推进工业设计的设计组织，是德国现代主义设计的基石，它在理论与实践上都为20世纪20年代欧洲现代主义设计运动的兴起和发展奠定了基础。其宗旨是通过艺术、工业和手工艺的结合，提高德国的设计水平，设计出优良的产品。

［4］brainstorm：集思广益，集体研讨。国内也常常翻译为"头脑风暴"，是当今最负盛名、最实用的一种集体式创造性解决问题的方法。

［5］UL：UL是英文Underwriter Laboratories Inc.（保险商试验所）的简写，是美国最有权威的，也是世界上从事安全试验和鉴定的较大的专业机构。它主要从事产品的安全认证和经营安全证明业务，其最终目的是为市场提供具有相当安全水准的商品。

［6］Jonathan Ive：乔纳森·伊夫，英国工业设计师，曾任Apple公司首席设计师兼资深副总裁，曾参与设计了iPod、iMac、iPhone、iPad等众多苹果产品。

［7］Phillipe Starck：菲利浦·斯塔克，法国人，世界著名设计大师，享有"设计鬼才""设计天才"、设计界"国王"等重量级美誉。他几乎囊括了所有国际性设计奖项，其中包括红点设计奖、IF设计奖、哈佛卓越设计奖等。

Exercises

Read the following statements carefully, and decide whether they are true (T) or false (F) according to the text.

1. Industrial design is a combination of aesthetics, ergonomics, business, and engineering.
2. It is a good idea to write down the solution to the problem at the problem assessment stage.
3. At the design specification stage, a list of requirements of everything should be written down including size of the object, what it should be made of and so on except a retail price.
4. Testing is a very essential part of product design and should not be neglected.
5. The product must be sent to a testing laboratory such as UL for a thorough testing by professionals.

Lesson 9 IDSA

The Industrial Designers Society of America (IDSA) is the world's oldest, largest, member-driven society for product design, industrial design, interaction design [1], ergonomics, design research, design management, universal design and related design fields. IDSA organizes the renowned Industrial Design Excellence Award (IDEA) [2] competition annually; hosts the International Design Conference and five regional conferences each year; and publishes *Innovation*, a quarterly on design, and *Designbytes*, a weekly e-newsletter [3] highlighting the latest headlines in the design world. IDSA's charitable arm, the Design Foundation, supports the dissemination of undergraduate scholarships annually to further industrial design education.

IDSA's logo

Carroll Gantz (FIDSA [4]) was president of IDSA from 1979—1980. Among his many contributions to the society, he provides the text for IDSA's online design history section, *100 Years of Design*.

The organization of professional designers can be traced to the beginning of the profession itself, which first came to the attention of the general US public in 1927. That year, Macy's in New York held a well-attended Exposition of Art in Trade. This featured 'modern products', many of them from the 1925 International Exposition of Modern Decorative and Industrial Arts [5] in Paris, which was belatedly recognized by the US government as an important 'modern movement'.

Immediate public and manufacturer demand for these new 'Art Deco' styles was so obvious, and the need so great, that a number of design professionals (often architects, package designers or stage designers) focused their creative efforts for the first time on mass-produced products. They claimed the new title of 'industrial designer' which had originated in the US Patent Office in 1913 as a synonym for the then-current term 'art in industry'.

Immediately, some of these professionals founded the American Union of Decorative Artists and Craftsmen (AUDAC) to protect their industrial, decorative and applied arts, and to exhibit their new work. AUDAC attracted a broad range of artists, designers, architects, commercial organizations, industrial firms and manufacturers. Within a few years, it had more than a hundred members, and held major exhibitions in 1930 and 1931.

In 1933, the National Furniture Designers' Council (NFDC) was founded, bringing together a number of furniture representatives and designers to draw up a code for the National Recovery Administration (NRA) to prevent design piracy. But in 1934, NRA was declared unconstitutional and NFDC disbanded.

In 1936, the American Furniture Mart in Chicago invited leading designers to form a new organization called the Designers' Institute of the American Furniture Mart. Some members felt restricted by the sole patronage and sponsorship of the furniture industry, and in 1938 they founded a broader-based organization called the American Designers Institute (ADI), which allowed specialization in one of many design areas, including crafts, decorative arts, graphics, products, packaging, exhibit or automotive styling, to name a few. ADI's first president was John Vassos.

In February 1944, fifteen prominent East Coast design practitioners established the Society of Industrial Designers (SID). Each of the founding members invited one additional designer to join the following year. Membership requirements were stringent, requiring the design of at least three mass-produced products in different industries. SID was formed in part to reinforce the legality of industrial design as a profession, and to restrict membership to experienced professionals. SID's first president was Walter Dorwin Teague [6].

In 1951, ADI relocated its administrative center to New York, absorbing the Chicago Society of Industrial Designers (CSID) in the process and changing its name to the Industrial Designers Institute (IDI). That year, IDI initiated annual national design awards, which continued through 1965. By 1962, IDI had about 350 members in 10 city chapters across the country.

In 1955, the Society of Industrial Designers (SID) changed its name to the American Society of Industrial Design (ASID). By 1962, ASID had about 100 members in four chapters nationally.

In 1957, the Industrial Design Education Association (IDEA) was founded because neither professional society (IDI or ASID) accepted educators as full members. Its first president was Joseph Carriero (1920—1978).

In 1965, after over ten years of careful negotiations, the Industrial Designers Society of America (IDSA) was formed by the collaborative merger of IDI, ASID and IDEA. In doing so, the strengths, purposes and varied philosophies of its predecessors combined to become the single voice of industrial design in the US.

Today, IDSA has over 3 300 members, 28 chapters, 17 special interest sections and over 30 student chapters in the US, UK and China. IDSA members frequently communicate with and interact with other corporations, design organizations and governments all over the world as a leader in the profession.

Herman Miller Ardea Light, IDEA 2010 Gold

Gateway One, IDEA 2010 Sliver

Background Information

　　IDSA：美国工业设计师协会，是美国工业设计师的专业组织，1965年由美国3个与工业设计相关的组织合并而成，它们分别是美国设计师协会（American Designers Institute, ADI）、全美工业设计师协会（American Society of Industrial Design, ASID）、美国工业设计教育联合会（Industrial Design Education Association, IDEA）。IDSA实行会员制，设七类会员，专业会员（professional member）、终身会员（life member）、特别会员（fellow member）、荣誉会员（honorary member）、国际会员（international member）、隶属会员（affiliate member）及独立学生会员（individual student member）。协会发行两份月刊，《创新杂志》（*Innovation Magazine*）和《设计视角》（*Design Perspectives*），并每年合订一本会员名册。IDSA下设的IDEA奖是全球工业设计界重要的评奖活动之一。

Words and Expressions

1. interaction [ˌɪntərˈækʃən] *n.* 相互影响，互动
2. ergonomics [ˌə:gəˈnɔmiks] *n.* 人机工程学，工效学
3. universal [ˌju:niˈvə:səl] *adj.* 通用的，万能的
4. renowned [riˈnaund] *adj.* 有名的，有声誉的
5. host [həust] *vt.* 主办
6. e-newsletter [ˈi:ˈnju:zˌletə] *n.* 电子刊物
7. highlight [ˈhailait] *vt.* 强调，突出
8. arm [ɑ:m] *n.* 部门，分部
9. predecessor [ˈpri:disesə] *n.* 前任，前身
10. belatedly [biˈleitidli] *adv.* 延迟地
11. package [ˈpækidʒ] *n.* 包装，包裹
12. patent [ˈpætənt] *n.* 专利

13. synonym ['sinənim] *n.* 同义词
14. representative [ˌrepri'zentətiv] *n.* 代表，代理人
15. piracy ['pairəsi] *n.* 剽窃，著作权侵害
16. unconstitutional ['ʌnˌkɔnsti'tju:ʃənəl] *adj.* 违反宪法的，违反章程的
17. disband [dis'bænd] *vt.* 解散
18. patronage ['pætrənidʒ, 'peitrənidʒ] *n.* 资助，赞助；支持
19. practitioner [præk'tiʃənə] *n.* 从业者
20. stringent ['strindʒənt] *adj.* 严厉的，严苛的
21. reinforce [ˌri:in'fɔ:s] *vt.* 加强，强化
22. chapter ['tʃæptə] *n.* （俱乐部、协会等的）支部，分会
23. negotiation [niˌgəuʃi'eiʃən] *n.* 协商

Notes

「1」interaction design：交互设计，是一种如何让产品易用、有效而使人愉悦的技术，致力于了解目标用户和他们的期望，了解用户在同产品交互时彼此的行为，了解"人"本身的心理和行为特点，同时还包括了解各种有效的交互方式，并对它们进行增强和扩充。

「2」Industrial Design Excellence Award：美国工业设计优秀奖，是由美国《商业周刊》（*Business Week*）主办、美国工业设计师协会IDSA担任评审的工业设计竞赛。该奖项设立于1979年，主要颁发给已经发售的产品，与德国的IF奖一样在世界上有着巨大的影响力。

「3」e-newsletter：电子报、电子刊物，指以电子邮件为主要传送方式的互联网络信息服务。近年来，随着互联网的普遍应用，e-newsletter逐渐流行并得到众多企业的认可和广泛应用。而对于用户来说，方便快捷、分类详细、内容出众的电子刊物也成为其猎取信息、学习知识的重要渠道。

「4」FIDSA：fellow membership of IDSA，美国工业设计师协会特别会员。

「5」International Exposition of Modern Decorative and Industrial Arts：即1925年在法国巴黎举办的世博会，主题是"装饰艺术与现代工业"。

「6」Walter Dorwin Teague：沃尔特·道文·提革，美国最早的职业工业设计师之一，1936年设计了柯达公司最早的便携式相机"班腾"相机，1955年设计了波音707大型喷气式客机。

Exercises

Choose the best answer to each question according to the text.
1. The term "industrial designer" had originated in _____.
A. the 1925 International Exposition of Modern Decorative and Industrial Arts

B. the US Patent Office in 1913 as a synonym for the then-current term 'art in industry'

C. a well-attended Exposition of Art in Trade held by Macy's in New York in 1927

2. The first president of the American Designers Institute was _____.

A. Carroll Gantz

B. John Vassos

C. Joseph Carriero

3. Partly in order to reinforce the legality of industrial design as a profession, and to restrict membership to experienced professionals, _____ was formed.

A. SID

B. ASID

C. ADI

4. The annual national design awards originated from _____.

A. CSID

B. IDI

C. IDEA

5. The Industrial Designers Society of America (IDSA) was formed by the collaborative merger of _____.

A. SID, IDI and IDEA

B. IDI, ADI and CSID

C. IDI, ASID and IDEA

Lesson 10　Environmental Design

We all know places where we would rather not reside or where we don't feel at home. Maybe it is because we don't like the architecture. Maybe because it is filthy and messy. Maybe because it has indoor air pollution. In fact it has become, unfortunately, a fact of life. Now the environmental design can solve the above problems.

Environmental design refers to the applied arts and sciences dealing with creating the human-designed environment. These fields include architecture, city planning (or urban planning), landscape architecture, and interior design. It can also encompass interdisciplinary areas such as historic preservation and lighting design. In terms of a larger scope, environmental design has implications for the industrial design of products: innovative automobiles, wind-electricity generators, solar-electric equipment, and other kinds of equipment could serve as examples. Currently, the term has expanded to apply to ecological and sustainability issues.

Ecological architecture 'Noah'

Landscape architecture designed by Chen Hongwei

The first traceable concepts of environmental design focused primarily on solar heating, which began in ancient Greece around 500 BCE[1]. At the time, most of Greece had exhausted its supply of wood for fuel, leading architects to design houses that would capture the solar energy of the sun. The Greeks understood that the position of the sun varies throughout the year. For a latitude of 40 degrees in summer the sun is high in the south, at an angle of 70 degrees at the zenith, while in winter, the sun travels a lower trajectory, with a zenith of 26 degrees. Greek houses were built with south-facing facades which received little to no sun in the summer but would receive full sun in the winter, warming the house. Additionally, the southern orientation also protected the house from the colder northern winds. This clever arrangement of buildings influenced the use of the grid pattern of ancient cities. With the north-south orientation of the houses, the streets of Greek cities mainly ran east-west.

The practice of solar architecture continued with the Romans, who similarly had deforested much of their native Italian Peninsula by the first century BCE. The Roman heliocaminus, literally 'solar furnace', functioned with the same aspects of the earlier Greek houses. The numerous public baths were oriented to the south. Roman architects added glass to windows to allow for the passage of light and to conserve interior heat as it could not escape. The Romans also used greenhouses to grow crops all year long and to cultivate the exotic plants coming from the far corners of the Empire. Pliny the Elder[2] wrote of greenhouses that supplied the kitchen of the Emperor Tiberius[3] during the year.

Along with the solar orientation of buildings and the use of glass as a solar heat collector, the ancients knew other ways of harnessing solar energy. The Greeks, Romans and Chinese developed curved mirrors that could concentrate the sun's rays on an object with enough intensity to make it burn in seconds. The solar reflectors were often made of silver, copper or polished brass.

Early roots of modern environmental design began in the late 19th century with writer/designer William Morris, who rejected the use of industrialized materials and processes in wallpaper, fabrics and books his studio produced. He and others, such as John Ruskin felt that the industrial revolution would lead to harm done to nature and workers.

The narrative of Phil Cousineau's documentary film *Ecological Design: Inventing the Future* asserts that in the decades after World War II, 'the world was forced to confront the dark shadow of science and industry'. From the middle of the 20th century, thinkers like Buckminster Fuller[4] have acted as catalysts for a broadening and deepening of the concerns of environmental designers. Nowadays, energy efficiency, appropriate technology, organic horticulture and agriculture, land restoration, New Urbanism[5], and ecologically sustainable energy and waste systems are recognized considerations or options and may each find application.

American museum in Montreal World Expo

By integrating renewable energy sources such as solar photovoltaic, solar thermal, and even geothermal energy into structures, it is possible to create zero emission buildings, where energy consumption is self-generating and non-polluting. It is also possible to construct 'energy-plus buildings' which generate more energy than they consume, and the excess could then be sold to the grid. In the United States, the LEED Green Building Rating System[6] rates structures on their environmental sustainability.

Examples of the environmental design process include use of roadway noise computer models in design of noise barriers and use of roadway air dispersion models in analyzing and designing urban highways. Designers consciously working within this more recent framework of philosophy and practice seek a blending of nature and technology, regarding ecology as the basis for design. Some believe that strategies of conservation, stewardship, and regeneration can be applied at all levels of scale from the individual building to the community, with benefit to the human individual and local and planetary ecosystems.

Background Information

environmental design：环境设计，又称"环境艺术设计"，是一种新兴的艺术设计门类。其包含的学科相当广泛，主要由建筑设计、城市规划设计、室内设计、公共艺术设计、景观设计等内容组成。

Words and Expressions

1. filthy ['filθi] *adj.* 肮脏的，污秽的
2. messy ['mesi] *adj.* 肮脏的；混乱的；麻烦的
3. indoor ['indɔ:] *adj.* 室内的，户内的
4. refer to 指的是；提及，涉及
5. landscape ['lændskeip] *n.* 景观，风景
6. interdisciplinary [,intə'disiplinəri] *adj.* 学科间，跨学科的，交叉学科的
7. in terms of 就……而言，在……方面
8. implication [,impli'keiʃən] *n.* 牵连；涉及；卷入
9. ecological [,ekə'lɔdʒikəl] *adj.* 生态的，生态学的
10. sustainability [sə,steinə'biliti] *n.* 持续性，能维持性，永续性
11. solar heating 太阳能供暖，太阳能加热
12. exhaust [ig'zɔ:st] *vt.* 用完，耗尽
13. capture ['kæptʃə] *vt.* 捕获

14. latitude ['lætitju:d] *n.* 纬度
15. zenith ['zi:niθ] *n.* 天顶
16. trajectory [trə'dʒektəri] *n.* 轨迹
17. facade [fə'sɑ:d] *n.* （建筑物的）正面，前面
18. grid [grid] *n.* 格子，网格
19. deforest [di:'fɔ:rist] *vt.* 砍伐森林
20. peninsula [pi'ninsjulə] *n.* 半岛
21. furnace ['fə:nis] *n.* 火炉，熔炉
22. greenhouse ['gri:nhaus] *n.* 温室
23. exotic [ig'zɔtik] *adj.* 外来的；奇异的
24. narrative ['nærətiv] *n.* 叙述，讲述
25. invent [in'vent] *vt.* 发明，创造
26. catalyst ['kætəlist] *n.* 催化剂
27. horticulture ['hɔ:tikʌltʃə] *n.* 园艺，园艺学
28. renewable [ri'nju:əbl] *adj.* 可更新的，可再生的
29. photovoltaic [,fəutəuvɔl'teik] *adj.* 光电的
30. thermal ['θə:məl] *adj.* 热的，热量的
31. emission [i'miʃən] *n.* 排放；散发；发行
32. rate [reit] *vt.* 评估，评价
33. stewardship ['stjuədʃip] *n.* 管理工作

Notes

「1」BCE：公元前，是Before the Christian Era的缩写形式。

「2」Pliny the Elder：指的是Gaius Plinius Secundus，即盖乌斯·普林尼·塞孔都斯（23或24—79），世称老普林尼（与其养子小普林尼相区别），古代罗马的百科全书式的作家，以其所著《自然史》一书著称。

「3」Emperor Tiberius：提比略（14—37），古罗马第二任皇帝。

「4」Buckminster Fuller：巴克明斯·福勒（1895—1983），美国思想家、哲学家、建筑家、工程师，代表作有节能多功能房、1967年蒙特利尔世博会美国馆等。

「5」New Urbanism：新城市主义，是20世纪90年代初提出的一个新的城市设计运动，主张借鉴二战前美国小城镇和城镇规划的优良传统，塑造具有城镇生活氛围的、紧凑的社区，取代郊区蔓延的发展模式。

「6」the LEED Green Building Rating System：LEED（Leadership in Energy and Environmental Design）是一个评价绿色建筑的工具。LEED由美国绿色建筑协会建立并于2003年开始推行，在美国部分州和一些国家已被列为法定强制标准，因此全称为Leadership in Energy and Environmental Design Building Rating System，简称为LEED。目前在世界各国的各类建筑环保评估、绿色建筑评估及建筑可持续性评估标准中，LEED被认为是最完善、最有影响力的评估标准。

Exercises

Read the following statemens carefully, and decide whether they are true (T) or false (F) according to the text.

1. In terms of a larger scope, environmental design which expanded to apply to ecological and sustainability issues include architecture, city planning, landscape architecture, interior design and industrial design of products.

2. The first solar architecture was designed by the Romans, who had deforested much of their native Italian Peninsula by the first century BCE.

3. From Pliny the Elder we can know that the Romans also used greenhouses to grow crops all year.

4. An energy-plus house produces more energy from renewable energy sources, on average over the course of a year, than it imports from external sources.

Lesson 11 Famous Interior Designers and Their Styles in Interior Design

The period of the 20th century was the time when famous interior designers started getting recognized by the public. In fact, the interior designing profession started gaining ground only in the later part of that century. Up until then, interior designing was a practically unknown industry. It can't be denied that the world of interior designing is not as prolific as the world of fashion for example. However, there are many enterprising, creative people who have made their mark as professional and influential interior designers. Several of them even design for the affluent, elite class of clients.

A number of famous interior designers in different parts of the globe have distinguished themselves by their unique style. One such designer is Nina Campbell[1].When Nina was twelve, she along with her mother would reposition furniture after having dinner. This uncontrollable habit probably contributed to Nina's talent for beautifying, revitalizing and decorating. Nina's career in the field of interior decoration took off when she worked for John Fowler[2] —a name associated with the famous wallpaper and fabric designing company—Colefax and Fowler[3]. Nina, whose mother was Viennese and father was Scottish, was brought up in a very cosmopolitan world. As a result, her style makes priorities of ease and luxury. 'I like mixing contemporary and traditional pieces, perhaps by teaming inherited furniture with new fabrics. I will always remember John Fowler at Colefax and Fowler saying:Don't decorate a room within an inch of its life. Give it space to breathe and have its own personality!', she said. Nina's style coupled with her sense of fabric and color helped her progress many steps forward in her career. Presently, Nina is one of the globe's leading interior designers and her range includes fabric, trimmings and wallpaper collections, and also collections of other items like furniture, table linen and gift wrap.

Nina Campbell   Nina Campbell's piece

Italian Mauro Lipparini[4] is another eminent interior designer. He is probably best known for his 'natural minimalism' style. Lipparini's style is characterized by wonderful touches of pleasure and joy. His use of bold colors and innovative visual ideas conveys several elements of the artistic. Lipparini has made several commendable contributions to the industrial design industry, including developing products for Japanese and European firms of high repute. Accolades that he has won in the course of his career include the International Du Pont Award Koln and the Young & Designer Milano.

Mauro Lipparini

Mauro Lipparinil's piece

Yet another well-known interior designer is Rachel Ashwell[5], popularly recognized as the owner and founder of Shabby Chic[6] and also the host of the TV program of the same name. 'Shabby Chic' is a term that reflects Ashwell's decorative tendencies. This includes providing the home with anything from antique furnishings to new tables, sofas, rugs and lamps. She gives importance to the cozy feel and also to flowers. Ashwell always goes for a combination of creams and whites; and light pinks, sea-foam greens and blues. Several top names in the celebrity business have benefited from Ashwell's exceptional designing talents, including singer Jennifer Lopez. Madonna, Anthony Hopkins and Julia Roberts are her other star status devotees.

Rachel Ashwell

Shabby Chic

Lesson 11 Famous Interior Designers and Their Styles in Interior Design

A celebrated name from the Middle East that has graced the interior design world and met the needs of the rich and famous is Israel-born Ron Arad[7]. Ron Arad achieved popularity in the 1980s for being a self-taught maker and designer of sculptural furniture. He is the creator of the Ron Arad Studio in Como[8], Italy and his works appear in many architectural and design publications across the world. He has also exhibited at a number of galleries and museums.

Ron Arad   Ron Arad's piece

Words and Expressions

1. recognize ['rekəgnaiz] vt. 承认，认可
2. gain ground 取得进展
3. prolific [prə'lifik] adj. 多产的，创作丰富的；丰富的，富饶的
4. enterprising ['entəˌpraiziŋ] adj. 有事业心的，有进取心的
5. mark [mɑ:k] n. 记号；痕迹
6. affluent ['æfluənt] adj. 富裕的
7. elite [ei'li:t] n. 精英，精华
8. distinguish [di'stiŋgwiʃ] vt. 区别，识别；使杰出，使显著
9. distinguish oneself （使自己）出名，受人注目
10. beautify ['bju:tifai] vt. 美化
11. revitalize [ˌri:'vaitəlaiz] vt. 使复兴，使恢复生气
12. decorate ['dekəreit] vt. 装饰，装潢
13. take off 起飞
14. cosmopolitan [ˌkɔzmə'pɔlitən] adj. 世界性的，国际性的
15. priority [prai'ɔriti] n. 优先，优先权
16. luxury ['lʌkʃəri] n. 奢侈，奢华
17. contemporary [kən'tempərəri] adj. 当代的

18. team [ti:m] vt. 使相配
19. within an inch of one's life 差点丧命
20. couple with 与……一起，连同
21. trimming ['trimiŋ] n. 装饰品
22. eminent ['eminənt] adj. 出众的，卓越的，著名的
23. commendable [kə'mendəbl] adj. 值得赞美的，值得称赞的
24. shabby ['ʃæbi] adj. 破烂的，破旧的
25. chic ['ʃi:k] adj. 时髦的，别致的
26. antique [æn'ti:k] adj. 古老的，陈旧的
27. cozy ['kəuzi] adj. 舒适的，惬意的
28. go for 竭力想取得；喜欢；适用于
29. celebrity [si'lebriti] n. 名人，名流
30. devotee [,devə'ti:] n. 热爱者，……迷
31. grace [greis] vt. 使增光

Notes

［1］Nina Campbell：妮娜·坎贝尔，英国人，国际著名的室内设计师，主要从事私人住宅、酒店和豪华游艇的室内装潢设计，同时设计印花面料及其他家居产品。在她的设计中，现代风格与传统风格融会贯通，演绎出了多姿多彩的融合，以舒适、高雅和独具古典魅力而闻名于世。

［2］John Fowler：约翰·福勒，英国著名的墙纸面料设计公司的创办人之一。

［3］Colefax and Fowler：英国著名的墙纸面料设计公司，是英式风格最好的代表，秉承着一贯优雅、微妙的特性，重点在于与舒适的完美结合和对品质的坚持。

［4］Mauro Lipparini：莫罗·里帕里尼，意大利著名设计师，被称为自然简约主义的倡导者和领军人物，其设计扎根于空间和形状，线条简约，有着强烈的生机蓬勃的气质。

［5］Rachel Ashwell：瑞秋·安斯韦尔，美国设计师，在20世纪90年代创造了Shabby Chic品牌的家居装饰方式。

［6］Shabby Chic：旧物别致风格，Shabby意为破旧的，Chic代表漂亮、时髦，两个单词组合在一起，代表着旧事物的时尚魅力。Shabby Chic的理念就是旧家具，即便是一些外表的织物和漆面已经有些破损的"古董"，也能变得非常漂亮和别致。作为一种家居装饰方式，Shabby Chic在美国流行已久，如今仍受到美国人的格外青睐，经久不衰。

［7］Ron Arad：路昂·阿拉德，著名的家具设计大师。阿拉德出生于以色列，后移居英国伦敦，1989年创立路昂·阿拉德设计事务所。

［8］Como：科莫，意大利北部阿尔卑斯山南麓城市，在科莫湖西南端、米兰以北40千米处。

Exercises

According to the pictures, translate the following passage into Chinese.

When you go inside from an amazing glassed entrance door, you will be surprised with the spectacular interior decoration of a grand living area with vaulted ceiling and exposed beams, marble fireplace, large bathroom, luxury marble countertops kitchen, walk-in dressing room and adjoining library, while the tiled floors flow through the living areas. The floor-ceiling windows are designed to allow the breathtaking views of the Kohala coast and Pacific, framed by mountains. Each master bedroom, guest bedroom and bathroom was set perfectly with beautiful ocean views from the windows.

Entrance door

Interior design

Living room design

Open-plan living area design

Master bedroom design

Kitchen design

Lesson 12 How to Become a Fashion Designer

Fashion design is a profession that tends to attract people at an early age. Someone who spends a large portion of their youth reading fashion magazines or making clothes for their dolls usually knows well before they become an adult that a career as a fashion designer has a particular appeal. However, there are many facets of the profession and many things to know about what it will take to forge a successful career in this field. This article provides an overview of the profession in terms of job duties, salary levels, and employment prospects; and it also reviews the skills, training, and other requirements needed to become a top-notch fashion designer.

What does a fashion designer do?

Fashion designers are the people who create the clothing and accessories purchased by the billions every year by the consumers. In doing this, designers regularly study fashion trends, sketch designs, select colors and fabrics, and oversee the process by which their original designs come to fruition in the form of new clothes and accessories. Some fashion designers specialize in clothing (men's, women's, and children's apparel), footwear (shoes and boots), or accessory (handbags, belts, scarves, hats, hosiery, etc.) design, whereas others create designs in all of these fashion categories.

Sketch design   Handbag

Depending on their experience level and also on the size of the design firm they work for, fashion designers may have varying levels of involvement in some or all of these process steps. Some fashion designers (about 25% of them) are self-employed. They generally work for individual clients on a contract. These types of designers tend to have sporadic working hours, often needing to make adjustments to their workday to suit their clients' schedules and deadlines. Other designers are employed by manufacturing establishments, wholesalers, or design firms, creating designs for the mass market. These types of designers generally tend to have a more normal work schedule, although even they will occasionally need to work long hours to meet production deadlines or prepare for fashion shows. The highest concentrations of fashion designers are employed in New York and California. The global nature of the industry requires constant interfacing with suppliers, manufacturers, and customers throughout the U.S. and the world, as well as regular attendance at trade and fashion shows. As a result, most fashion designers can expect frequent travel. Earnings in fashion design can vary widely based on the employer and years of experience. Beginning fashion designers, who usually start out as pattern makers[1] or sketching assistants for more experienced designers, tend to earn low salaries until becoming more established in the industry and advancing to higher level positions. Salaried designers as a rule earn higher and more stable incomes than self-employed designers. However, a small number of self-employed fashion designers who have become very successful earn many times the salary of even the highest paid salaried designers.

What steps should one follow to become a fashion designer?

Learn to draw and sew. Start at home by sketching some clothing ideas. Save these sketches and continually edit and revise them. Also learn about colors and how to mix them effectively. In addition to sketching ability, fashion designers also need to have sewing and patternmaking skills, even if they are not the ones who directly perform these tasks. Designers need to be able to understand these skills so they can properly oversee construction of garments. Also, designs will be more impressive if clients can see the finished item along with the sketch.

Patternmaking

Learn everything possible about the industry. Research companies that sell fashion and learn what type of fashion each company makes. Learn about fashion trends and try to predict what will be popular in the future. Learn the sales aspects of fashion, in terms of knowing the major department stores and the stores that sell specialty categories of fashion. Also become familiar with shopper profiles (age, income, lifestyles, etc.) and what customers are eager to buy.

Attend a school. Bachelors and associate degree programs in fashion design are offered at many colleges, universities, and private art and design schools. Plan to spend at least two years in any fashion design program. A list of accredited college-level programs can be obtained from the National Association of Schools of Art and Design. A very smart thing to do is to supplement a fashion design degree with a business, marketing, or fashion merchandising degree[2]. Strong sales and presentation skills and knowledge of the business end of the fashion industry are vital to a successful career.

Build a portfolio of original designs. A good portfolio of a person's best work is the best showcase of his/her creativity and can go a long way towards convincing potential employers that the person would be an asset to their business. The portfolio can be started at an early age, well before graduating from school, and should contain the widest variety of work possible.

Get industry experience any way possible. This can come at an early age in the form of volunteer work. Costuming for a community theater is one example of how to get started in the industry. An internship with a design or manufacturing firm will prove invaluable in terms of industry experience. A first job as a pattern maker or sketching assistant for more experienced designers may not pay handsomely but will be well worth the time spent in terms of preparation for moving up the career ladder.

How can a person become a GREAT fashion designer?

Develop a working knowledge of design-related software programs. In today's world, CAD software and programs such as Adobe Photoshop and Illustrator provide a vital capability to fashion designers. It is important to become familiar with as wide a variety of software programs as possible.

Subscribe to trade newspapers and fashion magazines. This is a great way to keep up-to-date with fashion trends. Industry professionals regularly tap into these publications and successful fashion designers should do the same.

Make as many industry connections as possible. Many of these relationships can be developed in school. Include people in related fields, such as advertising.

Qualifications to become a good fashion designer include a strong eye for color and detail, a sense of balance and proportion, and an appreciation for beauty. Fashion designers also need good communication and problem-solving skills, as well as sketching ability. But most important of all is knowing what the job entails and the steps one needs to take in order to be successful in this profession. A person who is armed with this knowledge is well ahead of the game in terms of career preparation and can look forward to embarking upon an interesting and rewarding career.

Lesson 12 How to Become a Fashion Designer

Background Information

fashion design：服装设计和其他设计行业一样，是系统性、综合性的设计活动。服装的款式、色彩和面料是服装设计的三大基本要素。结构设计、裁剪技术，也是服装设计师必须掌握的基础知识。此外，还要了解市场、了解消费者的购买心理，掌握当前的流行趋势，配合适当的行销途径，将服装通过销售转化为商品被消费者接受，真正体现其价值，才算成功完成了服装设计的全部过程。当今的服装设计师要能熟练地运用Photoshop、Coredraw、Painter、CAD等绘图软件，以熟练地编辑、修改和绘制图形，拓宽设计表现方式，加快设计速度。

Words and Expressions

1. doll [dɔl] *n.* 玩偶，洋娃娃
2. appeal [ə'pi:l] *n.* 吸引力，感染力
3. forge [fɔ:dʒ] *vt.* 锻炼，艰苦干成
4. accessory [ək'sesəri] *n.* （衣服的）配饰
5. oversee [ˌəuvə'si:] *vt.* 监督，管理
6. come to fruition 实现，完成
7. apparel [ə'pærəl] *n.* 衣服，服装
8. scarves [skɑ:vz] *n.* （scarf的复数形式）围巾，披巾；领带
9. self-employed [ˌself im'plɔid] *adj.* 自己经营的，个体经营的
10. sporadic [spə'rædik] *adj.* 偶尔发生的
11. establishment [i'stæbliʃmənt] *n.* 企业，机构
12. mass [mæs] *n.* 大众，民众
13. concentration [ˌkɔnsen'treiʃən] *n.* 浓度，含量；集中
14. start out 开始
15. revise [ri'vaiz] *vt.* 修改
16. garment ['gɑ:mənt] *n.* 服装
17. department store 百货公司
18. eager ['i:gə] *adj.* 热切的，渴望的
19. supplement ['sʌplimənt] *vt.* 补充，增加
20. portfolio [pɔ:t'fəuliəu] *n.* 作品选辑
21. asset ['æset] *n.* 资产，财产
22. volunteer [ˌvɔlən'tiə] *n.* 志愿者
23. internship ['intə:nʃip] *n.* 实习，见习
24. handsomely ['hænsəmli] *adv.* 大方的，慷慨的；可观的
25. ladder ['lædə] *n.* 梯子，阶梯
26. subscribe [səb'skraib] *vi.* 订阅，订购
27. up-to-date ['ʌp tə 'deit] *adj.* 最新的
28. tap into 深入，进一步了解

29. appreciation [ə,pri:ʃi'eiʃən] n. 鉴赏，欣赏
30. be armed with 用……装配，用……武装
31. embark [im'bɑ:k] vi. 从事，着手

Notes

「1」pattern maker：样板师，主要工作职责是把设计师的设计图纸打样、制版，被视作"把设计理念转化为可操作实现的承上启下的灵魂人物"。

「2」fashion merchandising degree：时装营销采购学位，即学习时装、零售、销售及国际市场行销等一系列商务课程，以培养创造性和商务头脑来开拓时装市场，使时装不只是呆在设计师的陈列室中，而是能够流向零售业。

Exercises

I. Read the following statements carefully, and decide whether they are true (T) or false (F) according to the text.

1. All fashion designers specialize in clothing, footwear and accessory design.
2. Fashion design beginners tend to earn low salaries when they usually start out as pattern makers or sketching assistants for more experienced designers.
3. Fashion designers need to have more sewing and patternmaking skills, sketching ability than strong sales, presentation skills and knowledge of the business end of the fashion industry.
4. A first job as a pattern maker or sketching assistant for more experienced designers will prove invaluable in terms of industry experience.

II. Topic for oral discussion.

Talk about how to become a great fashion designer.

Lesson 13 The History of Animation

Animation is a word that has practically stormed the film industry these days. Everyone, right from the 8-year-old kids to the 80-year-old granddads, loves to watch an animation flick. Have you ever wondered what animation exactly is and how did it come into existence? Animation is basically the rapid display of a sequence of images, of 2-D or 3-D artwork or model positions. The display is so rapid that it creates an illusion of movement in the viewers. The phenomenon of persistence of vision [1] is the main basis behind the development of animation. In case you want to further explore the origin and history of animation, make use of the information provided in the lines below.

The earliest instance of animation dates back to the Paleolithic times, when attempts were made to capture motion in drawings. The cave paintings of that time depict animals in superimposed positions, drawn with an aim of conveying the perception of motion. Persistence of vision, the basis behind animation, was discovered by Ptolemy, the Greek astronomer, in 130 AD. Fifty years later, in 180 AD, an unknown Chinese inventor created an early animation device, which we later came to know as the zoetrope [2].

Phenakistoscope [3], praxinoscope [4] and the flip book [5] are the other early animation devices, which were invented during the 1800s. All these devices made use of technological means for the purpose of producing movement from sequential drawings. However, it was the introduction of motion picture films, in the late 1890s that gave a boost to the concept of animation. There is no single person who can be credited with the title of the 'creator' of animation. This is because when animation was developed, many people were involved in the same thing at the same time.

Phenakistoscope

Praxinoscope

J. Stuart Blackton [6] was the first person to make an animated film, which he called 'humorous phases of funny faces'. For the purpose, he used to draw comical faces on a blackboard, one after the other, and film them. In 1910, Emile Cohl [7] came out with the first paper cutout animation. The development of celluloid, around 1913, made animation much easier to manage. While talking about the history of animation, three names that are definitely worth mentioning are those of Winsor McCay [8] of the United States, and Emile Cohl and Georges Melies [9] of France.

Emile Cohl's *Fantasmagorie* (1908) was the first animated film that was made using 'traditional (hand-drawn) animation'. Georges Melies, a creator of special-effect films, was the first person to use animation, along with special effects. He was the one who gave the idea of stop-motion animation [10]. Winsor McCay also created a number of animation films, with the most noted ones being *Little Nemo* (1911), *Gertie the Dinosaur* (1914) and *The Sinking of the Lusitania* (1918). In fact, many people take *The Sinking of the Lusitania* to be the first animated feature film.

J. Stuart Blackton

The Post of *Gertie the Dinosaur*

However, it was Walt Disney [11] who took animation to an entirely new level altogether. In 1928, with the premiere of *Steamboat Willie*, he became the first animator to add sound to his movie cartoons. Walt Disney achieved another milestone in 1937, when he produced the first full length animated feature film, named *Snow White and the Seven Dwarfs*. The year 1955 saw Art Clokey producing *Gumby*, a stop-motion clay animation. Introduction of computers marked a step further in the concept of animation.

Lesson 13 The History of Animation

Walt Disney

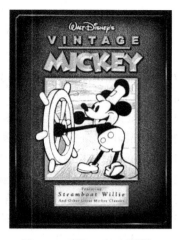

The post of *Steamboat Willie*

In 1951, an MIT[12] student Ivan Sutherland created a computer drawing program, *Sketchpad*, further giving a boost to animation. With time, computer started gaining an increasing importance in the field of animation. Movies like *Star Wars* relied on computer animation for many of its special effects. In 1995 came *Toy Story*, produced by Walt Disney Productions and Pixar Animation Studios[13], the first full length feature film animated totally on computers. Since that time, animation and computer have gone hand in hand, creating new milestones with time.

Background Information

animation:"动画"一词的英文有animation、cartoon、animated cartoon、cameracature。其中,比较正式的"animation"一词源自于拉丁文字根anima,意思为"灵魂",动词animate的意思是"赋予生命",引申为使"某物活起来"的意思。手绘动画、定格动画与计算机动画共同构成了现代动画的三大门类。

Words and Expressions

1. flick [flik] *n.* (俚语)电影
2. a sequence of 一连串,一系列
3. illusion [i'luːʒən] *n.* 错觉,幻觉
4. in case 如果,以防
5. instance ['instəns] *n.* 例子,实例
6. date back to 追溯到,从……开始
7. paleolithic [ˌpeiliə'liθik] *adj.* 旧石器时代的
8. cave painting 洞穴壁画
9. superimpose [ˌsuːpərim'pəuz] *vt.* 重叠,叠加
10. perception [pə'sepʃən] *n.* 感知,知觉
11. zoetrope ['zəuiˌtrəup] *n.* 西洋镜

12. phenakistoscope [ˌfenə'kistəskəup] *n.* 费纳齐镜，转盘活动影像镜
13. motion picture 电影
14. boost [buːst] *n.* 推动，帮助，促进
15. comical ['kɔmikəl] *n.* 滑稽的，好笑的
16. celluloid ['seljuˌlɔid] *n.* 电影胶片
17. milestone ['mailstəun] *n.* 里程碑，转折点
18. dwarf [dwɔːf] *n.* 矮子，有魔法的小矮人
19. animate ['ænimeit] *vt.* 绘制（卡通影片）
20. hand in hand 手拉手，密切合作

Notes

［1］ the phenomenon of persistence of vision：视觉暂留现象，也可称为duration of vision。人眼在观察景物时，光信号传入大脑神经，需经过一段短暂的时间，光的作用结束后，视觉形象并不立即消失，这种残留的视觉称"后像"，视觉的这一现象则被称为"视觉暂留"。

［2］ zoetrope：西洋镜，一种民间的游戏器具，匣子里面装着画片儿，匣子上放有放大镜，根据光学原理暗箱操作可以看放大的画面。因为最初画片多是西洋画，所以叫西洋镜。

［3］ phenakistoscope：费纳齐镜，早期的动画装置，由尤瑟夫·普拉托和他的儿子发明。两个圆盘装在一个支架上，前面的盘子边上有开口，后面的盘子上有一系列图画。让这些图画和开口连起来，透过这些开口看转动的盘子就有运动的效果。

［4］ praxinoscope：普拉克辛视镜/实用镜。1877年由法国人埃米尔·雷诺发明，他通过在一条30英尺长的叫作"晶体"的透明薄膜上画画产生一系列短的强烈动作的效果。

［5］ the flip book：手翻书。1868年在全世界出现了一种叫"翻页本"的玩具，它非常简单但广受欢迎。手翻书是将一沓画着图画的纸订在一起的小书，手抓住装订的一头，另一只手可以翻动页面，这样就看到了画面在运动。

［6］ J. Stuart Blackton：詹姆斯·斯图尔特·布莱克顿（1875—1941），出生于英国，后移民美国，在1906年制作了美国第一部动画片。

［7］ Emile Cohl：爱米尔·科尔（1857—1938），法国漫画家、卡通动画制作者，被称为"现代动画之父"，1908年创作了动画影片《幻影集》。

［8］ Winsor McCay：温瑟·马凯（1871—1934），美国知名的专业漫画家与插画家，创作了《小尼莫梦境历险》《蚊子的故事》《恐龙葛蒂》《路斯坦尼雅号之沉没》等一系列卡通影片。

［9］Georges Melies：乔治·梅里爱（1861—1938），法国人，被誉为"电影之父"。

［10］stop-motion animation：逐格动画，也称为"定格动画"，是通过逐格地拍摄对象，然后使之连续放映，从而产生仿佛活了一般的人物或所能想象到的任何奇异角色。通常所指的定格动画一般都是由黏土偶、木偶或混合材料做成的角色来演出的。

［11］Walt Disney：华特·迪士尼（1901—1966），美国著名导演、制片人、编剧、配音演员和卡通设计者，并且和其兄洛伊·迪士尼一同创办了世界著名的华特迪士尼公司。

［12］MIT：Massachusetts Institute of Technology的缩写，即麻省理工学院，是当今世界上最负盛名的大学之一。

［13］Pixar Animation Studios：皮克斯动画工作室，总部坐落于美国加利福尼亚州的爱莫利维尔市，一直致力于制作优秀的计算机动画作品，公司的作品多次获得奥斯卡最佳动画短片奖、最佳动画长片奖及其他技术类奖项。

Exercises

Choose the best answer to each question according to the text.

1. The phenomenon of persistence of vision which is the main basis behind the development of animation was discovered by _____.

A. Ptolemy, the Greek astronomer

B. Georges Melies, a creator of special-effect films

C. J. Stuart Blackton, the first person to make an animated film

2. The following are the early animation devices which were invented during the 1800s except _____.

A. praxinoscope

B. zoetrope

C. sketchpad

3. _____ who took animation to an entirely new level altogether was the first animator to add sound to his movie cartoons.

A. Walt Disney

B. Art Clokey

C. Emile Cohl

Lesson 14 The History of Photoshop

In September 1988, the Knoll brothers' luck changed. John presented a demo[1] to Adobe's internal creative team, and they loved the product. A license agreement was struck soon after, and Photoshop 1.0 was shipped in February 1990 after 10 months of development.

Thomas has remained involved with the project all along. He never did have time to finish his thesis. John has continued his career at ILM[2], serving as visual effects supervisor on projects such as *'Mission Impossible'*(1996),*'Star Trek: First Contact'*(1996), and *'Star Wars: Episode I - The Phantom Menace'*(1999). Glenn Knoll[3] is still working as a professor for the College of Engineering at the University of Michigan. But he now uses a Powerbook G3[4] at home. And the darkroom in the basement has since been replaced by, yes, you guessed it, Photoshop.

John Knoll

Thomas Knoll

In the beginning

By 1987, John Knoll was working at Industrial Light and Magic — Lucasfilm's nascent special effects division, founded for *Star Wars* — while Thomas was studying for his Ph.D. on image processing at the University of Michigan. Having just bought a brand-new Apple Mac Plus to help out with his thesis, he was dismayed to find it couldn't display greyscale images on the monochrome monitor. So, in true hacker style, he set about writing his own code to do the job.

Unsurprisingly, John was also working on image processing at ILM, and during a holiday visit he became very impressed with Thomas's progress. In the book *CG 101: A Computer Graphics Industry Reference*, John says, 'As Tom showed me his work, it struck me how similar it was to the image-processing tools on the Pixar[5].'Thus the pair began to collaborate on a larger, more cohesive application, which they dubbed — excitingly —Display.

It wasn't long before John had bought a new colour Macintosh II and persuaded Thomas to rewrite Display to work in colour. Indeed, the more John saw of Display, the more features he began to ask for: gamma correction[6], loading and saving other file formats, and so on.

Although this work distracted Thomas from his thesis, he was quite happy to oblige. He also developed an innovative method of selecting and affecting only certain parts of the image, as well as a set of image-processing routines — which would later become plug-ins. A feature for adjusting tones (Levels) also emerged, along with controls for balance, hue and saturation. These were the defining features of Photoshop, but at the time, it was almost unthinkable to see them anywhere outside of specialist processing software in a lab — or at ILM.

By 1988, Display had become ImagePro and was sufficiently advanced that John thought they might have a chance at selling it as a commercial application. Thomas was reluctant: he still hadn't finished his thesis, and creating a full-blown application would take a lot of work. But once John had checked out the competition, of which there was very little, they realised ImagePro was way ahead of anything currently available.

From ImagePro to Photoshop

Thus the search began for investors. It didn't help that Thomas kept changing the name of the software, only to find a name was already in use elsewhere. No one is quite sure where the name 'Photoshop' originally came from, but legend has it that it was suggested by a potential publisher during a demo, and just stuck. Incidentally, splash screens[7] from very early versions show the name as 'Photoshop' — which seems far more in line with today's craze for extraneous capitalization.

Remarkably in retrospect, most software companies turned their corporate noses up at Photoshop, or were already developing similar applications of their own. Only Adobe was prepared to take it on, but a suitable deal wasn't forthcoming. Eventually, though, a scanner manufacturer called Barneyscan decided to bundle it with its scanners, and a small number of copies went out under the name Barneyscan XP[8].

Fortunately for the future of digital imaging, this wasn't a long-term deal, and John soon returned to Adobe to drum up more interest. There he met Russell Brown, then Art Director, who was highly impressed with the program and persuaded the company to take it on. Whether through naivety on Adobe's part or canniness on the brothers', Photoshop was not sold wholesale but only licensed and distributed, with royalties still going to the Knolls.

It wasn't as if this deal meant the Knoll brothers could sit back and relax; if anything, they now had to work even harder on getting Photoshop ready for an official, 1.0 version release. Thomas continued developing all the main application codes, while John contributed plug-ins separately, to the dismay of some of the Adobe staff who viewed these as little more than gimmicks[9].

Curiously, this attitude still remains among some purists, who claim that most Photoshop plug-ins are somehow 'cheating' and not be touched under any circumstances, while others swear by their flexibility and power when used properly.

As in the program's formative days, there were always new features to be added, and somehow Thomas had to make time to code them. With the encouragement of John, Russell Brown — soon to become Photoshop's biggest evangelist — and other creatives at Adobe, the application slowly took shape. It was finally launched in February 1990.

Photoshop 1.0

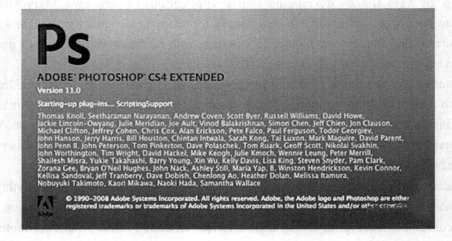

Photoshop CS4 (11.0)

Lesson 14　The History of Photoshop

Background Information

Photoshop：Adobe Photoshop是Adobe公司旗下最为出名的图像处理软件之一，其创作者是美国的托马斯·诺尔（Thomas Knoll）和约翰·诺尔（John Knoll）兄弟，如今已渗透到数字生活的方方面面。这款软件诞生仅仅20余年，在多年的时间里，Photoshop改变了人们认识世界、感知现实、表达自我的方式。环顾四周，几乎所有图片，无论是广告、宣传栏，还是报纸、杂志上的图片都或多或少地使用了Photoshop编辑加工。

Words and Expressions

1. demo ['deməu] *n.* 演示版
2. license ['laisns] *n.* 许可，特许；许可证，执照
3. thesis ['θi:sis] *n.* 论文，毕业（或学位）论文
4. nascent ['næsnt] *adj.* 初期的，开始形成的
5. division [di'viʒən] *n.* 部门
6. Ph.D. *abbr.* 博士学位
7. dismay [dis'mei] *vt.* 使沮丧，使气馁
8. greyscale [grei'skeil] *n.* 灰阶，灰度
9. monochrome ['mɔnəkrəum] *adj.* 单色的，黑白的
10. hacker ['hækə] *n.* 黑客；计算机高手
11. cohesive [kəu'hi:siv] *adj.* 有结合性的，有凝聚性的
12. dub [dʌb] *vt.* 把…称为，给…取绰号
13. gamma correction　伽马校正
14. distract [di'strækt] *vt.* 转移，分散；使分心
15. oblige [ə'blaidʒ] *vi.* 帮忙，效劳
16. plug-in ['plʌg,in] *n.* 插件，外挂程序
17. emerge [i'mə:dʒ] *vi.* 出现
18. saturation [,sætʃə'reiʃən] *n.* 饱和度
19. reluctant [ri'lʌktənt] *adj.* 不情愿的，勉强的
20. full-blown ['ful'bləun] *adj.* 完善的，成熟的
21. legend ['ledʒənd] *n.* 传说
22. in line with　和……一致，符合
23. extraneous [eks'treiniəs] *adj.* 外来的
24. inherent [in'hiərənt] *adj.* 固有的，内在的
25. capitalization [,kæpitəlai'zeiʃən] *n.* 资本化
26. retrospect ['retrəu,spekt] *n.* 回想，回顾
27. turn one's nose up at　对……嗤之以鼻
28. forthcoming [,fɔ:θ'kʌmiŋ] *adj.* 即将到来的，唾手可得的
29. drum up　竭力争取
30. naivety [nɑ:'i:vti] *n.* 天真

31. canniness ['kæninis] n. 精明
32. royalty ['rɔiəlti] n. 专利权税，版税
33. if anything 如果有区别的话，如果有什么的话
34. gimmick ['gimik] n. 花招
35. purist ['pjuərist] n. 纯粹主义者
36. flexibility [,fleksə'biliti] n. 灵活性
37. launch [lɔ:ntʃ] vt. 发行，推出，投放市场

Notes

［1］demo：demo是demonstration的缩写，原意为"示范""展示""样片""样稿"，在软件版本中，demo即为演示版，一般分两种：一种是功能齐全但有时间限制，大多为30天，30天过后就会要求使用者通过购买才能继续使用；另一种是在正式版出来前提供的体验版，这种版本没有时间限制，但大多功能不完整。

［2］ILM：全称Industrial Light and Magic，即工业光学魔术公司，简称工业光魔。由好莱坞著名导演乔治·卢卡斯（George Lucas）于1981年正式创立，是目前全球第一大特效制作公司，《星球大战》《珍珠港》《加勒比海盗》《侏罗纪公园》《变形金刚》等著名影片都是ILM的作品。

［3］Glenn Knoll：格伦·诺尔，诺尔兄弟的父亲。

［4］Powerbook G3：是苹果电脑公司在1997—2000年期间生产的笔记本。

［5］Pixar：皮克斯，全名为皮克斯动画工作室（Pixar Animation Studios），于1986年正式成立，至今已经出品11部动画长片和19部动画短片，是继迪士尼公司之后对动画电影历史影响最深远的公司。公司于2006年被迪士尼收购，成为其全资子公司。

［6］gamma correction：伽玛校正，是对图像的伽玛曲线进行编辑，以对图像进行非线性色调编辑的方法，检出图像信号中的深色部分和浅色部分，并使两者比例增大，从而提高图像对比度效果。

［7］splash screen：splash原意为"溅、泼"，splash screen通常是指计算机软件的启动画面或是快闪窗口。

［8］Eventually, though, a scanner manufacturer called Barneyscan decided to bundle it with its scanners, and a small number of copies went out under the name Barneyscan XP：然而最终，一个名为Barneyscan的扫描仪制造商决定将它与扫描仪捆绑在一起，以Barneyscan XP的名字卖出了少量。当诺尔兄弟寻找投资者时，多数硅谷公司并不看好这款软件，均拒绝投资。最终，一家小型幻灯片扫描仪开发商Barneyscan同意签定短期授权合同，当时的Photoshop软件被命名为Barneyscan XP，仅售出约200套。

［9］Adobe的一些人认为John的插件过于花俏，不适合于严肃的应用程序。他们的观点是他们的产品仅作为一种润饰的工具，而非为了特殊作用，所以John只能偷偷地把这些

插件编写进去，正是这些原来为很多人所不齿的插件，却成为日后Photoshop成功的一大因素。时至今日，插件已经成为Photoshop不可或缺的重要功能。

Exercises

Translate the following passage into Chinese.

Though Adobe Photoshop is an investment of several hundreds of dollars, this robust, image-editing software is a popular choice for graphic artists, web designers and photographers. The program features a variety of functions that you can use to manipulate photos or create new images. For its many functions, many professionals understand Photoshop's high cost to be an investment.

Color Correction

Photoshop is equipped with several tools, like burn, sponge and dodge, that are utilized for detailed color correction. Dodge, for example, lightens parts of an image, while sponge reduces the contrast and saturation. With these tools, you can make color corrections that don't necessarily apply to an entire image. This program also supports a function for color-to-black-and-white conversion, with which you can adjust and save your preferences for the tone and tint of the image.

Selection Functions

Photoshop has selection tools that permit users to quickly and easily select different parts of an image. For example, if you want to select the tie someone is wearing in a photograph, you can use the magnetic lasso tool that 'reads' the image and adheres to the outline of the tie. Selecting specific parts of an image like this enables you to make individual changes — in this example, you could easily change the color of the tie without affecting the rest of the image.

Lesson 15 Dreamweaver and It's Advantages

Adobe Dreamweaver (formerly Macromedia Dreamweaver) is a web development application originally created by Macromedia [1], and is now developed by Adobe Systems, which acquired Macromedia in 2005.

Dreamweaver is a web page design program that lets you type text and add media elements directly into a page, much as you would with a word processing program like Microsoft Word. It converts your text and graphical page design into the HTML [2] code read by a Web browser and is available for both Mac and Windows operating systems. Recent versions have incorporated support for web technologies such as CSS [3], JavaScript [4], and various server-side scripting languages and frameworks including ASP [5], ColdFusion [6], and PHP [7].

It allows users to preview websites in locally installed web browsers. It provides transfer and synchronization features, the ability to find and replace lines of text or code by search terms and regular expressions across the entire site, and a templating feature that allows single-source update of shared code and layout across entire sites without server-side includes or scripting. The behaviours panel also enables use of basic JavaScript without any coding knowledge, and integration with Adobe's Spry Ajax [8] framework offers easy access to dynamically-generated content and interfaces.

Dreamweaver can use third-party 'Extensions' to extend core functionality of the application, which any web developer can write (largely in HTML and JavaScript). Dreamweaver is supported by a large community of extension developers who make extensions available (both commercial and free) for most web development tasks from simple rollover [9] effects to full-featured shopping carts [10].

Dreamweaver is a highly interactive web page editor which enables you to build websites that are highly dynamic without having to know HTML or code anything. However, experienced users can make use of codes if this is what they prefer. If you learn Dreamweaver skills such as 'drag-and-drop', the work of making websites becomes very easy. A graphical user interface allows the user to construct highly advanced websites which make use of very complex scripting technologies.

Here is a brief summary of some of the elements that Dreamweaver offers:

Site Management — An integrated file transfer client and visual site map allow site navigation, file linking, and uploading/ synchronization of your site.

Template — Templates allow users to quickly edit all common elements, such as navigation bars, throughout a whole site.

Cascading Style Sheets — CSS allow users to quickly change the appearance of text elements throughout the site.

JavaScript Behaviors — Dreamweaver behaviors are JavaScripts that you can apply without having to deal with the necessary code.

Background Information

Adobe Dreamweaver：Dreamweaver是集网页制作和管理网站于一身的所见即所得的网页编辑器，它是第一套针对专业网页设计师特别开发的视觉化网页开发工具，利用它可以轻而易举地制作出跨越平台限制和跨越浏览器限制的充满动感的网页。

Words and Expressions

1. acquire [ə'kwaiə] vt. 获得，得到
2. convert [kən'və:t] vt. 转变，变化
3. graphical ['græfikəl] adj. 图形的，图像的
4. code [kəud] n. 代码
5. browser ['brauzə] n. 浏览器
6. available [ə'veiləbl] adj. 可用的
7. incorporate [in'kɔ:pəreit] vt. 加上，包含
8. server-side n. 服务器端
9. script [skript] n. 脚本
10. preview ['pri:vju:] n. 预看，预览
11. synchronization [,siŋkrənai'zeiʃən] n. 同步
12. template ['templit] n. 模板
13. enable [i'neibl] vt. 使能够，使成为可能
14. integration [,inti'greiʃən] n. 集成
15. extend [iks'tend] vt. 扩展，延伸
16. shopping cart 购物车
17. interactive [,intər'æktiv] adj. 相互作用的，交互的
18. dynamic [dai'næmik] adj. 动态的
19. navigation [,nævi'geiʃən] n. 导航
20. upload [ʌp'ləud] vt. 上传

Notes

「1」Macromedia：软件开发设计公司，总部设立在美国加州旧金山，在全球50多个国家设有经营机构。Macromedia公司的软件产品被全球数以百万计的开发人员和设计人员所使用，为他们提供了高效地创造互联网上最为有效的用户体验，于2005年被Adobe公司收购。

「2」HTML：全称为Hyper Text Mark-up Language，即超文本标记语言或超文本链接标示语言，是目前网络上应用最为广泛的语言，也是构成网页文件的主要语言。

〔3〕CSS：Cascading Style Sheet，可译为"层叠样式表"或"级联样式表"，是一组用于控制Web页面外观的格式设置规则。通过使用CSS样式设置页面的格式，可将页面的内容与表现形式分离，页面内容存放在HTML文件中，而用于定义表现形式的CSS规则则存放在另一个文件中或HTML文件的某一部分，通常为文件头部分。

〔4〕JavaScript：JavaScript是一种基于对象和事件驱动并具有相对安全性的客户端脚本语言，同时也是一种广泛用于客户端Web开发的脚本语言，常用来给HTML网页添加动态功能，如响应用户的各种操作。

〔5〕ASP：ASP是Active Server Page的缩写，意为"动态服务器页面"。ASP是微软公司开发的一种简单、方便的编程工具，网页文件的格式是.asp，现在常用于各种动态网站中。

〔6〕ColdFusion：是一种Web应用开发、服务提供和管理的集成环境。

〔7〕PHP：是英文超级文本预处理语言Hypertext Preprocessor的缩写，是一种在服务器端执行的嵌入HTML文件的脚本语言。

〔8〕Adobe's Spry Ajax：Ajax是由Jesse James Garrett创造的名词，是指一种创建交互式网页应用的网页开发技术。Adobe's Spry Ajax是Adobe公司针对目前越来越流行的Ajax技术而推出的自己的Ajax框架。

〔9〕rollover：指的是当移动光标经过图形或是单击该图形时，浏览器中的图形改变其外观，这种效果包括按钮和替换图案。

〔10〕shopping carts：在本文中是指能够建立、执行及管理网上商店的功能。

Exercises

Read the following statements carefully, and decide whether they are true (T) or false (F) according to the text.

1. Dreamweaver is a web page design program that is only available for Mac operating systems.

2. Integration with Adobe's Spry Ajax framework, the behaviours panel also enables use of basic JavaScript without any coding knowledge, and offers easy access to dynamically-generated content and interfaces.

3. People who don't know HTML or code anything can make use of Dreamweaver to build a highly interactive web page.

Unit Three

Design Masters

Lesson 16 World Graphic Design Master: Paul Rand

Paul Rand was a well-known American graphic designer, best known for his corporate logo designs. Rand was educated at the Pratt Institute [1] (1929—1932), the Parsons School of Design [2] (1932—1933), and the Art Students League[3] (1933—1934). He was one of the originators of the Swiss Style[4] of graphic design. From 1956 to 1969, and beginning again in 1974, Rand taught design at Yale University in New Haven, Connecticut. Rand was inducted into the New York Art Directors Club Hall of Fame[5] in 1972. He designed many posters and corporate identities, including the logos for IBM, UPS and ABC[6]. Rand died of cancer in 1996.

When Paul Rand died at age 82, his career had spanned six decades and numerous chapters of design history. His efforts to elevate graphic design from craft to profession began as early as 1932, when he was still in his teens. By the early 1940s, he had influenced the practice of advertising, book, magazine, and package design. By the late 1940s, he had developed a design language based purely on form where once only style and technique prevailed.

Paul Rand

Early life and education

Peretz Rosenbaum[7] was born in Brooklyn, New York in 1914. As Orthodox Jewish law forbids the creation of graven images that can be worshiped as idols, Rand's career creating icons venerated in the temple of global capitalism seemed as unlikely as any. It was one that he embraced at a very young age, painting signs for his father's grocery store as well as for school. Rand's father did not believe art could provide his son with a sufficient livelihood, and so he required Paul to attend Manhattan's Harren High School while taking night classes at the Pratt Institute, though 'neither of these schools offered Rand much stimulation'. Despite studying at

Pratt and other institutions in the New York area (including Parsons School of Design and the Art Students League), Rand was by-and-large 'self-taught as a designer, learning about the works of Cassandre[8] and Moholy-Nagy from European magazines such as *Gebrauchsgraphik* [9]'.

Early career

His career began with humble assignments, starting with a part-time position creating stock images for a syndicate that supplied graphics to various newspapers and magazines. In his early twenties he was producing work that began to garner international acclaim, notably his designs on the covers of *Direction* magazine, which Rand produced for no fee in exchange for full artistic freedom.

Although Rand was most famous for the corporate logos he created in the 1950s and 1960s, his early work in page design was the initial source of his reputation. In 1936, Rand was given the job of setting the page layout for an *Apparel Arts* magazine anniversary issue.'His remarkable talent for transforming mundane photographs into dynamic compositions, which gave editorial weight to the page' earned Rand a full-time job, as well as an offer to take over as art director for the *Esquire-Coronet* magazines at the young age of twenty-three.

Corporate identities

Indisputably, Rand's most widely known contribution to graphic design are his corporate identities, many of which are still in use. IBM, ABC, Cummins Engine, Westinghouse, and UPS, among many others, owe their graphical heritage to him, though UPS recently carried out a controversial update to the classic Rand design. One of his primary strengths, as Moholy-Nagy pointed out, was his ability as a salesman to explain the needs his identities would address for the corporation.

Rand's defining corporate identity was his IBM logo in 1956, which as Mark Favermann notes 'was not just an identity but a basic design philosophy that permeated corporate consciousness and public awareness'. The logo was modified by Rand in 1960, and the striped logo in 1972. Rand also designed packaging and marketing materials for IBM from the early 1970s until the early 1980s, including the well known Eye-Bee-M poster.

IBM Logo

Eye-Bee-M Poster

Dada Poster

Development of theory

Rand soon became known not only for his design, but also for his philosophy of design. Though Rand was a recluse in his creative process, doing the vast majority of the design load despite having a large staff at varying points in his career, he was very interested in producing books of theory to illuminate his philosophies.

As is obvious, Dewey[10] is an important source for Rand's underlying sentiment in graphic design; on page one of Rand's groundbreaking *Thoughts on Design*, the author begins drawing lines from Dewey's philosophy to the need for 'functional-aesthetic perfection' in modern art. Among the ideas Rand pushed in *Thoughts on Design* was the practice of creating graphic works capable of retaining their recognizable quality even after being blurred or mutilated, a test Rand routinely performed on his corporate identities.

Rand left behind a huge legacy for professionals. During the final decade of his life he published three important books, *Paul Rand: A Designer's Art,* (1985), *Design Form and Chaos* (1994), and *From Lascaux to Brooklyn* (1996). Not just retrospectives, these books codified the principles he adhered to in his professional life.

Background Information

Arts and Crafts Movement：保罗·兰德（1914—1996），是当今美国乃至世界上最杰出的图形设计师、思想家及设计教育家之一。保罗·兰德一生创作范围相当广泛，涉及了书籍装帧设计、广告海报、插图、字体设计和企业形象设计等多个领域，他为世界知名公司和机构所设计的企业标志，已成了家喻户晓的经典之作。对设计的独到理解使得兰德获得了社会的一致好评，作品被欧美和日本的多家博物馆收藏，他也因其作品而获得艺术指导俱乐部、耶鲁大学、哈佛大学等授予的多项荣誉。保罗·兰德的作品设计风貌不拘一格，富于变化、且具有强烈的现代感。构图严谨、线面简洁的抽象几何图形，承袭了"包豪斯"设计哲学的理性之美。而自由、敏感的具象造型及鲜明强烈的色彩运用，又赋予其作品清新隽永的幽默感及独特情思，画面洗练而韵味无穷。

Words and Expressions

1. induct [in'dʌkt] *vt.* 吸收……为会员
2. poster ['pəustə] *n.* 招贴，海报
3. span [spæn] *vt.* 横跨，跨越
4. elevate ['eliveit] *vt.* 提高，提升
5. prevail [pri'veil] *vi.* 流行，盛行
6. orthodox ['ɔ:θə,dɔks] *adj.* 正统的，传统的
7. Jewish ['dʒu:iʃ] *adj.* 犹太人的，犹太教的
8. worship ['wə:ʃip] *vt.* 崇拜，敬仰
9. idol ['aidl] *n.* 偶像
10. venerate ['venə,reit] *vt.* 尊敬，崇拜
11. embrace [im'breis] *vt.* 欣然接受
12. sufficient [sə'fiʃənt] *adj.* 足够的，充分的
13. stimulation [,stimju'leiʃən] *n.* 刺激，激励，启发，鼓舞
14. by-and-large 大体上，总的来说
15. humble ['hʌmbl] *adj.* 卑微的，低下的
16. stock [stɔk] *n.* 股票
17. syndicate ['sindikit] *n.* 财团，企业联合组织
18. garner ['gɑ:nə] *vt.* 取得，获得
19. logo ['lɔgəu] *n.* 标志，商标
20. apparel [ə'pærəl] *n.* 衣服，服装
21. anniversary [,æni'və:səri] *adj.* 周年的，周年纪念的
22. mundane ['mʌndein] *adj.* 平凡的，平淡的
23. dynamic [dai'næmik] *adj.* 有活力的，有生气的
24. controversial [,kɔntrə'və:ʃəl] *adj.* 争议的，争论的
25. point out 指出，指明
26. permeate ['pə:mieit] *vt.* 渗入，渗透
27. strip [strip] *vt.* 成条状，成带状
28. recluse [ri'klu:s] *n.* 独居者，隐居者，隐士
29. underlying [,ʌndə'laiiŋ] *adj.* 基本的，根本的
30. sentiment ['sentimənt] *n.* 观点，看法
31. groundbreaking ['graund,breikiŋ] *adj.* 开创性的
32. blur [blə:] *vt.* 使模糊不清
33. mutilate ['mju:tileit] *vt.* 使残缺不全，使支离破碎

Notes

［1］the Pratt Institute：普拉特学院，是由查尔斯·普拉特（Charles Pratt）在1887年所创立的一所私立艺术学院，许多世界著名的艺术家、设计家和建筑师等都是该校的毕业生。目前的三所分校分别坐落在美国纽约州的曼哈顿、布鲁克林区及尤蒂卡。普拉特学院是美国居于领军层次的艺术类院校之一，也是美国设计与艺术学院协会（AICAD）的成员。

［2］the Parsons School of Design：帕森斯设计学院，位于纽约的帕森斯设计学院于1896年成立，是享誉世界的设计学院。

［3］the Art Students League：纽约艺术学生联盟，是一所于1875年在美国纽约市曼哈顿成立的艺术学校，创立的目的是为了弥补当时国家设计学院（National Academy of Design）课程上面弹性和种类的不足，希望提供校外人士及对艺术有喜好的人一个长期进修的场所。

［4］Swiss Style：瑞士平面设计风格，20世纪50年代期间，一种崭新的平面设计风格在联邦德国与瑞士形成，被称为"瑞士平面设计风格"（Swiss Design）。由于这种风格简单明确，传达功能准确，很快流行全世界，成为二战后影响最大、国际最流行的设计风格，因此又被称为"国际主义平面设计风格"（the International Typographic Style）。

［5］the New York Art Directors Club Hall of Fame：纽约艺术指导俱乐部名人堂。艺术指导俱乐部于1920年在纽约创立，是一个在广告、平面设计、多媒体、摄影、插图、广播设计、字体及相关领域的国际性非营利性创作机构，任务是推广视觉传递中最高水准的优秀设计及鼓励学生与年轻专业人士进入这个领域。自1971年起推出"Hall of Fame（名人堂）"表彰那些在艺术指导与视觉传达方面具有卓越成就的创意人，他们都代表着其一生对创意领域具有贡献的创新者。

［6］IBM, UPS and ABC：分别为美国的国际商业电器公司（International Business Machines Corporation）、联合包裹服务公司（United Parcel Service）和美国广播公司（American Broadcasting Company）的缩写。

［7］Peretz Rosenbaum：保罗·兰德的本名，为避免本名过于犹太风格，增强姓名的辨识度，将名字缩短为Paul，改用舅舅的姓氏Rand，创造了前后都是4个字母的新名字。

［8］Cassandre：卡桑德拉（1901—1968），法国画家、商业海报艺术家和字体设计师。

［9］Gebrauchsgraphik：德语，杂志名《实用绘图》。

［10］Dewey：约翰·杜威（John Dewey，1859—1952），美国著名哲学家、教育家，实用主义哲学的创始人之一。

Exercises

Read the following statements carefully, and decide whether they are true (T) or false (F) according to the text.

1. The works of Cassandre and Moholy-Nagy had an important influence on Paul Rand.

2. Corporate identities made Paul Rand earn the initial reputation.

3. After taking over as art director for the *Esquire-Coronet* magazines, Rand was given the job of setting the page layout for an *Apparel Arts* magazine anniversary issue.

4. As an excellent graphic designer, Rand was not only interested in design, but also in illuminating his philosophy of design.

Lesson 17 Raymond Loewy — the Man Who Streamlined the Sales-Curve

Raymond Loewy, born on the 5th of November 1893 in Paris and died on the 14th of July 1986 in Monaco, counts to the best known pioneers of the American industrial design of the twentieth century. His creation was stamped by a symbiosis of simplicity, functionality, very best quality and elegance. Countless articles of daily use, means of transportation as well as logo types count to his works. Still today the design of the legendary S1 steam locomotive is classified as a landmark of design and a perfect example of the streamline.

Raymond Loewy   1949 Cover Character of *Time*

Loewy studied at Lycée Chaptal[1] and began an engineer's course which he had to break off in 1914 because of the First World War. After the war he emigrated to the US and worked as his first and only salaried employment as a shop-window decorator for Saks[2] and Macy's[3].

Till 1929 he earned his money as a free illustrator for some fashion magazines. Although trained as an engineer, the job was temporarily right to combine his sense of style with his training as an engineer. Finally, in 1929 he became the Art Director of the Westinghouse Electric Company[4] and soon opened his own office where he founded his legendary career as an industrial designer.

'Between two products equal in price, function, and quality, the better looking will outsell the other.' He proved that the success of a product is as dependent on aesthetics as on function. 'The goal of design is to sell', he said. And to drive the point home, he added, 'the loveliest curve I know is the sales curve'.

The first years of the worldwide economic crisis about 1930 were not easy. And his first job was to redesign a duplicator — it was an unsightly copying machine, typical for manufactured products at this time, and actually it was so constructed that it only fulfilled the purpose of copying. It dawned on Loewy that the clumsy construction held optical and functional defects as well as danger potential — particularly the protruding thin legs were a prime example of bad industrial design. Thus he quickly draw a sketch showing the stumbling over the bulky thing and thus all documents flying around in space. This seemed to have convinced the client.

In 1930 the opportunity to put his dream of automobile design into action was close. The Hupp Motor Car Corporation suffered from bad turnovers and a revolutionary, extremely progressive car-design seemed a good means to master the crisis. Thus the economic situation helped to entrust rather unknown Loewy to design a new generation of Hupmobiles. The design of the 1932 Hupmobile striked an aesthetic concept which expressed plainness and simplicity. Exceedingly smooth and even forms suggested quickness as well as movement that has become known as the streamline style. Its most important characteristics are the closed, streamlined forms that strongly suggest speed, symbolic of the dynamism of modern times.

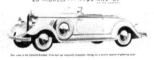

1932 Hupmobile

Raymond Loewy was also active as a design consultant who created the corporate image of numerous firms. From 1935 Raymond Loewy received several commissions for redesigning large department stores. He designed new packaging for Lucky Strike cigarettes, the Coca-Cola and Shell logos and the famous Coca-Cola bottle is a signature of Loewy's design. Raymond loewy said, 'the coke bottle is the most perfectly designed package in the word'. He redesigned the famous bottle in 1954. His contribution to that particular icon was to 'slenderize' the already existing version, giving it a more refined silhouette and making it sexier to a new generation.

Lucky Strike　　　　　　　　　　　　Coca-Cola

Shell Logo

During the 1960s and 1970s, Raymond Loewy advised US administrations, redesigning the airplane Air Force One[5] for John F. Kennedy. It was Raymond Loewy who inspected the interior of Skylab for NASA[6] to evaluate the quality of life astronauts would have in it (1969—1972). Ramond Loewy's philosophy of design, summed up in the acronym MAYA (most advanced, yet acceptable), was the main factor ensuring the success of so many of his designs. Published in 1951, Raymond Loewy's autobiography, '*Never Leave Well Enough Alone*', was an international best seller.

Lesson 17 Raymond Loewy — the Man Who Streamlined the Sales-Curve

Raymond Loewy with Air Force One

Background Information

Raymond Loewy：雷蒙德·罗维，20世纪最著名的工业设计师，设计行业的先锋者。他首开工业设计的先河，促成设计与商业的联姻；并凭借敏锐的商业意识、无限的想象力与卓越的设计禀赋为工业的发展注入鲜活的生命元素。其设计数目之多，范围之广令人瞠目：大到汽车、宇宙空间站，小到邮票、口红、公司的标志。罗维的设计生涯一直持续到80多岁高龄，作为美国工业设计的奠基人，他的一生伴随着美国工业设计从开始、发展直至顶峰并逐渐衰退的过程，因此被冠予"工业设计之父"的称号，无论20世纪中期的美国人意识到与否，他们实际生活在雷蒙德·罗维的世界之中。

Words and Expressions

1. streamline ['stri:mlain] *vt.* 使……成流线型
2. Monaco ['mɔnəkəu] *n.* 摩纳哥
3. symbiosis [ˌsimbai'əusis] *n.* 共生，共栖，互生
4. article ['ɑ:tikl] *n.* 用品
5. legendary ['ledʒəndəri] *adj.* 传说的，传奇的
6. break off *vt.* 中断，中止；突然停止
7. emigrate ['emigreit] *vt.* 移居，移民
8. Art Director 艺术总监
9. outsell [aut'sel] *vt.* 比……卖得多
10. drive the point home 讲透彻，使理解
11. duplicator ['dju:plikeitə] *n.* 复印机
12. unsightly [ʌn'saitli] *adj.* 难看的，不悦目的
13. clumsy ['klʌmzi] *adj.* 笨拙的，制作粗陋的
14. optical ['ɔptikəl] *adj.* 眼睛的，视觉的
15. defect [di'fekt] *n.* 缺点，缺陷，不足之处

15. protrude [prə'tru:d] *vi.* 伸出，突出
16. stumble ['stʌmbl] *vi.* 绊脚，绊倒
17. bulky ['bʌlki] *adj.* 体积庞大的，笨重的
18. turnover ['tə:n,əuvə] *n.* 营业额，交易额
19. entrust [in'trʌst] *vt.* 委托
20. even ['i:vən] *adj.* 平坦的，平滑的
21. dynamism ['dainəmizəm] *n.* 精力，活力
22. slenderize ['slendəraiz] *vt.* 使变细，使看起来苗条
23. silhouette [,silu'et] *n.* 轮廓；剪影
24. acronym ['ækrənim] *n.* 首字母缩略字
25. best seller *n.* 畅销书，畅销商品

Notes

〔1〕Lycée Chaptal：法语，夏普达尔高中。

〔2〕Saks：Saks Fifth Avenue，萨克斯第五大道精品百货店，是世界上顶级的百货公司之一，从1824年以来一直为纽约市民提供高品质的服饰及服务。在全球有50多家门店，旗舰店位于纽约第五大道。

〔3〕Macy's：梅西百货公司，是纽约市最老牌的百货公司，坐落于曼哈顿中城第三十四街与百老汇街、第七大道的交接处，是纽约人与观光客的汇集之地。1994年被美国联合百货公司收购。

〔4〕Westinghouse Electric Company：西屋电气公司，世界著名的电工设备制造企业。1886年1月8日，由乔治·威斯汀豪斯在美国宾夕法尼亚州创立，总部设在宾夕法尼亚州匹兹堡市。

〔5〕Air Force One：空军一号，是美国总统的专机，这架蓝白相间的波音747飞机已成为美国的权力象征。

〔6〕NASA：美国国家航空航天局（National Aeronautics and Space Administration），是美国负责太空计划的政府机构，总部位于华盛顿哥伦比亚，拥有最先进的航空航天技术，为人类探索太空做出巨大贡献。

Exercises

Choose the best answer to each question according to the text.

1. Raymond Loewy created his brilliant career as an industrial designer when_____.

A. he redesigned a duplicator in 1930

B. he became the Art Director of the Westinghouse Electric Company and soon opened his own office in 1929

C. he designed a new generation of Hupmobiles for the Hupp Motor Car Corporation in

1932

2. From this sentence 'the loveliest curve I know is the sales curve', we can learn that Raymond Loewy's philosophy of design is_____.

A. the streamline style

B. pay more attention to function than appearance

C. in pursuit of the combination of design and business

3. Loewy redesigned a duplicator in order to_____.

A. make it fulfill the purpose of copying

B. make documents fly around in space

C. make it achieve the perfect combination of function and appearance

4. Which of the following is not the design works of Raymond Loewy?_____.

A. The Westinghouse logo

B. The Coca Cola and Shell logos

C. The Coca Cola bottle

Lesson 18 Frank Lloyd Wright and His Architectures

Believing that 'the space within that building is the reality of that building'[1], Frank Lloyd Wright (1867—1959) was one of the most prolific and influential architects of the 20th century. From his early Prairie Style[2] homes, to the sculptural curves of the Guggenheim Museum[3] in New York he defined a North American style of architecture which was rich in emotion and sensitive to its surroundings.

Frank Lloyd Wright

Guggenheim Museum

One of the founders of modern architecture in North America, Frank Lloyd Wright embraced the use of new technology, materials and engineering to create some of the 20th century's most influential and iconic buildings. During a long and productive career spanning 70 years he designed over 1 000 buildings of which over 400 were built.

Born in 1867, Wright was the eldest child of William Russell Cary Wright, a Unitarian minister and music teacher, and Anna Lloyd Jones Wright. His father gave him a love of music, but it was his mother who encouraged him to become an architect. As well as hanging prints of cathedrals on his bedroom wall, she bought him a Frederick Froebel[4] Kindergarten system on a visit to the Philadelphia Centennial in 1876. This system consisted of a set of coloured strips of paper, two dimensional geometric grids and a set of wooden bricks comprising cubes, spheres and pyramids. Later Wright wrote 'the maple wood blocks…. all are in my fingers to this day'. An infinite and playful combination of these geometric shapes gave Wright the core forms of his architecture.

At 18, Wright enrolled to study engineering at the University of Wisconsin[5], Madison but, desperate to pursue a career in architecture, he dropped out and moved to Chicago where he quickly found work with the architectural firm of Joseph Lyman Silsbee. Wright's ambition, however, soon took him to Adler[6] and Sullivan[7], Chicago's most progressive architects. Louis Sullivan was an important influence on Wright and put him in charge of the firm's residential building work. He also gave him a loan in 1889 to purchase land to build a home for himself and his new wife, Catherine Lee Tobin, in the Oak Park district of Chicago. In 1893 Wright was asked to leave the firm for pursuing too much private work and at the age of 26 he started his own practice.

During the next 16 years Wright developed the Prairie Style of architecture in a large number of commissions for private homes in Chicago, in particular, in Oak Park. It is to his credit that most of his clients were extremely pleased with the homes Wright built. One of his less published achievements was his mastery of the internal environment, with great attention paid to lighting, heating and climate control. The Prairie Style aimed to create a truly North American architecture, but Wright also drew inspiration from Europe: from the French rationalist writings of Eugene Viollet-le-Duc and the British Arts and Crafts movement. He also had great knowledge of the art and architecture of Japan and the culture of pre-Columbian America.

The 1906 Robie House in Chicago was Wright's most mature expression of the Prairie Style of architecture. Frederick Robie, an engineer and industrialist, wanted a house full of light with views of the street, but without his neighbours looking in. Using brick, concrete, steel and glass, Wright constructed a massive cantilever on the west side of the house that gave the living room privacy and shelter from the sun. It also opened out the house by moving away from the tight box shape of traditional homes. The low, horizontal form is exaggerated with the use of ribbons of cream stone for the base plinth and copingstones and red brick for the walls. A central fireplace open above the mantel gave greater unity of space to the large living and dining rooms, which Wright saw as the centre of family life. Although there was no external garden, the use of massive planters and urns softened the hard edges of the building and at each level Wright designed a terrace, balcony or porch to break the division between inside and outside. All internal details — including the furnishings, light fittings, rugs and the essential art glass — were also designed by Wright.

Robie House

Fallingwater

Most of Wright's residential commissions in this period were for middle-income professionals such as teachers and journalists, with a few from self-made businessmen like Frederick Robie. The 1935 commission for Fallingwater[8] at Mill Run, Pennsylvania from Edgar J. Kaufmann was an exception and resulted in Wright's most imaginative solution for a residential commission which is among his most famous buildings.

Frank Lloyd Wright died in 1959 at the age of 92. Despite the lulls and even great dips in his career he had continued designing and building for 70 years and at his death he left a thriving practice[9]. Unlike many architects who perhaps are remembered for a distinct decade of work Wright was able to adapt as his architecture moved with the changing requirements of a fast-moving century. He used the newest materials and technologies from poured concrete to under floor heating and was happy to design for all incomes. He was also a romantic who wanted to charge his work with emotional qualities. A house as a home for a family was an almost sacred place with the heat of a fire at its heart[10]. Indeed it is his romantic and emotional response to architecture and its environment that makes Wright's work seem particularly relevant today.

Background Information

1. Frank Lloyd Wright：弗兰克·劳埃德·赖特，美国著名建筑师，在世界上享有盛誉。赖特对现代建筑有很大的影响，他的建筑空间灵活多样，既有内外空间的交融流通，同时又具备安静隐蔽的特色。他既运用新材料和新结构，又始终重视和发挥传统建筑材料的优点，并善于把两者结合起来。同自然环境的紧密配合则是他建筑作品的最大特色。赖特的主要作品有：东京帝国饭店、流水别墅、约翰逊蜡烛公司总部、西塔里埃森、古根海姆美术馆、普赖斯大厦、唯一教堂、佛罗里达南方学院教堂等。

Words and Expressions

1. prolific [prə'lifik] adj. 多产的；丰富的
2. prairie ['prɛəri] n. 大草原，牧场
3. sculptural ['skʌlptʃərəl] adj. 雕刻的，雕刻般的
4. iconic [ai'kɔnik] adj. 符号的，图表的；标志性的
5. unitarian ['juːniˈtɛəriən] n.（认为上帝只有一位的）唯一神教派
6. minister ['ministə] n. 牧师，神职人员
7. kindergarten ['kɪndəˌɡɑːtn] n. 幼儿园
8. Philadelphia [ˌfɪləˈdelfjə] n. 费城
9. centennial [sen'tenjəl] n. 百年纪念
10. strip [strip] n. 条，带，细长片
11. geometric [dʒiə'metrik] adj. 几何的
12. brick [brik] n. 积木

13. pyramid ['pirəmid] *n.* 棱锥（体）
14. maple ['meipl] *n.* 枫树
15. enroll [in'rəul] *vi.* 入学，登记
16. drop out 离开，退出，退学
17. ambition [æm'biʃən] *n.* 雄心，抱负
18. loan [ləun] *n.* 贷款
19. rationalist ['ræʃənəlist] *n.* 理性主义者
20. mature [mə'tjuə] *adj.* 成熟的
21. industrialist [in'dʌstriəlist] *n.* 企业家，实业家
22. concrete ['kɔnkri:t] *n.* 混凝土
23. massive ['mæsiv] *adj.* 巨大的；大量的
24. cantilever ['kæntili:və] *n.* 悬臂
25. shelter ['ʃeltə] *vt.* 遮蔽，掩蔽
26. horizontal [,hɔri'zɔntl] *adj.* 水平的，横的
27. exaggerate [ig'zædʒəreit] *vt.* 夸张，夸大；使扩大
28. ribbon ['ribən] *n.* 带，带状物
29. plinth [plinθ] *n.* 基座，基脚
30. copingstone ['kəupiŋ,stəun] *n.* （建）盖顶石；墩台石
31. mantel ['mæntəl] *n.* 壁炉架，壁炉台
32. external [eks'tə:nl] *adj.* 外部的，外面的
33. planter ['plɑ:ntə] *n.* 花盆，花架
34. urn [ə:n] *n.* 瓮，缸
35. terrace ['terəs] *n.* 露台，平台屋顶
36. balcony ['bælkəni] *n.* 阳台
37. self-made ['self'meid] *adj.* 白手起家的，靠自己努力而成功的
38. lull [lʌl] *n.* 平静时期，暂停，间歇
39. dip [dip] *n.* （暂时的）下跌，下降
40. sacred ['seikrid] *adj.* 神圣的，庄严地

Notes

「1」the space within that building is the reality of that building：建筑物的内部空间是建筑物的主体，这是赖特关于他的有机建筑理论的著名观点。他认为建筑之所以为建筑，其实质在于它的内部空间。赖特主张设计每一个建筑，都应该根据各自特有的客观条件，形成一个理念，把这个理念由内到外，贯穿于建筑的每一个局部，使每一个局部都互相关联，成为整体不可分割的组成部分。

「2」Prairie Style：草原风格，是赖特于1900年前后设计的一系列住宅，建筑从实际生活需要出发，在布局、形体，以至取材上，特别注意同周围自然环境的配合，建筑外观高低错落，坡屋顶悬挑很远，在墙上投下大片暗影。形成以横线条为主的构图，舒展安

定，既具有美国建筑的传统风格，又突破了传统建筑的封闭性，形成了一种具有浪漫主义闲情逸致及田园诗意般的典雅风格。

〔3〕Guggenheim Museum：古根海姆博物馆，该博物馆是索罗门·R·古根海姆（Solomon R.Guggenheim）基金会旗下所有博物馆的总称，它是世界上最著名的私人现代艺术博物馆之一，也是全球性的一家以连锁方式经营的艺术场馆。

〔4〕Frederick Froebel：弗里德里希·福禄贝尔（1782—1852），德国教育家，现代学前教育的鼻祖，他不仅创办了第一所称为"幼儿园"的学前教育机构，他的教育思想迄今仍在主导着学前教育理论的基本方向。福禄贝尔运用自己在数学和建筑学方面的专长，为儿童设计了6套玩具，以球、立方体和圆柱体为基本形态，供儿童触摸、抓握，被称为"福禄贝尔教具"。

〔5〕the University of Wisconsin：威斯康辛大学，坐落于美国密歇根湖西岸的威斯康辛州，首府麦迪逊市，是一所有着超过150年历史的全美最顶尖的三所公立大学之一。

〔6〕Adler：大卫·阿德勒（1882—1949），出生于威斯康辛州，建筑师，大部分时间都在芝加哥从事家庭居所的建筑设计，作品优雅而实用。

〔7〕Sullivan：路易斯·沙利文（1856—1924），美国现代建筑（特别是摩天楼设计美学）的奠基人、芝加哥学派的中坚人物。

〔8〕Fallingwater：流水别墅，别墅主人为匹兹堡百货公司老板德国移民考夫曼，故又称考夫曼住宅。现代建筑的杰作之一，别墅外形强调块体组合，使建筑带有明显的雕塑感。两层巨大的平台高低错落，一层平台向左右延伸，二层平台向前方挑出，几片高耸的片石墙交错着插在平台之间，很有力度，内外空间互相交融，浑然一体。流水别墅在空间的处理、体量的组合及与环境的结合上均取得了极大的成功，为有机建筑理论作了确切的注释，在现代建筑历史上占有重要地位。

〔9〕at his death he left a thriving practice：在他逝世后，他还有一个蓬勃发展的实践尚未完成。指的是美国的古根海姆博物馆，是赖特晚年的杰作，1959年古根海姆博物馆对外开放时，赖特已经去世半年多了。

〔10〕A house as a home for a family was an almost sacred place with the heat of a fire at its heart：在核心空间有壁炉的一所房子对于一个家庭来说是近乎神圣的地方。在赖特的建筑里，中心壁炉就是一所房子的心脏，代表着家庭的凝聚力，给建筑带来了一种厚重感。

Exercises

Topic for oral discussion.

Talk about your view on the North American style of architecture developed by Frank Lloyd Wright.

Lesson 19 Fashion Queen — Coco Chanel

'Perishable trend, style last forever.'

— Coco Chanel

Gabrielle Bonheur Chanel was a pioneering French fashion designer whose modernist philosophy, menswear-inspired fashions, and pursuit of expensive simplicity made her an important figure in 20th century fashion. She was the founder of the famous fashion brand Chanel. Her extraordinary influence on fashion was such that she was the only person in the field to be named on *Time* 100: The Most Important People of the Century[1].

Coco Chanel and her little black dress

Coco Chanel Logo

Chanel was born on 19 August 1883 in the small town of Saumur France. She was the second daughter of Albert Chanel and Jeanne Devolle, a market stallholder and laundrywoman respectively at the time of her birth. Her birth was declared the following day by employees of the hospital in which she was born. They, being illiterate, could not provide or confirm the correct spelling of the surname and it was recorded by the mayor François Poitou as 'Chasnel'. This misspelling made the tracing of her roots almost impossible for biographers when Chanel later rose to prominence. She had five siblings: two sisters and three brothers.

In 1895, when she was 12 years old, Chanel's mother died of tuberculosis and her father left the family a short time later because he needed to work to raise his children. Because of his work, the young Chanel spent six years in the orphanage of the Roman Catholic monastery of Aubazine, where she learned the trade of a seamstress. School vacations were spent with relatives in the provincial capital, where female relatives taught Coco to sew with more flourish than the nuns at the monastery were able to demonstrate. Chanel's early years tended to be vague in detail. It is generally accepted that Chanel gained some dressmaking and millinery experience prior to working in a hat shop in Deauville[2], France. Using her skills as a milliner she opened shops in Paris, Deauville, and Biarritz[3] with the financial assistance of a backer. Chanel was an astute businesswoman and skillful publicist, quickly expanding her work to include skirts, jerseys and accessories.

Recognized as the designer of the 1920s, Chanel initiated an era of casual dressing, appropriate to the occasion, for relaxed outdoor clothing created to be worn in comfort and without constricting corsets, liberating women with loosely fitting garments. Her style was of uncluttered simplicity, incorporating practical details.

Highly original in her concept of design, Chanel ceaselessly borrowed ideas from the male wardrobe, combining masculine tailoring with women's clothing. Her suits were precise but remain untailored, with flowing lines, retaining considerable individuality and simple elegance. Riding breeches, wide-legged trousers, blazers, and sweaters were all taken and adapted. Chanel's coordination of the cardigan, worn with a classic straight skirt, became a standard combination of wearable separates.

Her colors were predominantly grey, navy, and beige, incorporating highlights of a richer and broader palette. Chanel introduced the ever popular 'little black dress', created for daywear, eveningwear, and cocktail dressing which became a firm fixture in the fashion world during her tenure, and is still popular today.

Attentive to detail, adding to day near and eveningwear, Chanel established a reputation for extensive uses of costume jewelry, with innovative combinations of real and imitation gems, crystal clusters, strings of pearls, and ornate jewelled cuff links, adding brilliant contrast to the stark simplicity of her designs. The successful development of Chanel No. 5 perfume in 1922 assisted in the financing of her couture empire during difficult years. An interesting aspect of Chanel's career was the reopening of her couture house, which was closed during World War II. After 15 years, Chanel relaunched her work in 1954 at the age of 71, reintroducing the Chanel suit, which formed the basis for many of her collections and become a hallmark. The look adopted shorter skirts and braid trimmed cardigan jackets.

Tweed suit

Chanel No. 5 perfume

Chanel craved personal and financial independence, and was ruthless in her search for success. She was unique in revolutionizing the fashion industry with dress reform and in promoting the emancipation of women. Her influence touched many American and European designers, who have continued to reinforce her concept of uncomplicated classics. Once such designer is Karl Lagerfeld[4] who took over designing the Chanel couture line in 1983 and its ready-to-wear collections the following year. He is widely credited with bringing Chanel back to the forefront of fashion, by taking original Chanel designs and tweaking them to appeal to younger customers.

Background Information

Coco Chanel：可可·香奈儿（1883—1971），原名加布里埃·邦思·香奈儿，著名时装设计师，于1913年在法国巴黎创立香奈儿品牌。香奈儿的产品种类繁多，有服装、珠宝饰品、配件、化妆品、香水，每一种产品都闻名遐迩，特别是她的香水与时装。香奈儿时装永远有着高雅、简洁、精美的风格，可可善于突破传统，早在20世纪40年代就成功地将女装推向简单、舒适，设计了不少创新的款式，如针织水手裙、黑色迷你裙、套装等。而且，可可从男装上取得灵感，一改当年女装过分艳丽的绮靡风尚。

Words and Expressions

1. extraordinary [ik'strɔ:dənəri] *adj.* 特别的，非凡的
2. stallholder ['stɔ:l,həuldə] *n.* 摊贩，租用摊位者
3. laundrywoman ['lɔ:ndri,wumən] *n.* 洗烫衣服的女工
4. illiterate [i'litərit] *adj.* 文盲的，未受教育的
5. biographer [bai'ɔgrəfə] *n.* 传记作者
6. prominence ['prɔminəns] *n.* 卓越，杰出，声望
7. sibling ['sibliŋ] *n.* 兄弟姐妹
8. tuberculosis [tju:,bə:kju'ləusis] *n.* 肺结核
9. orphanage ['ɔ:fənidʒ] *n.* 孤儿院
10. monastery ['mɔnəstəri] *n.* 修道院
11. seamstress ['si:mstris] *n.* 女裁缝师
12. relative ['relətiv] *n.* 亲属，亲戚
13. flourish ['flʌ:riʃ] *n.* 花饰
14. nun [nʌn] *n.* 修女
15. vague [veig] *adj.* 模糊的，不明确的，不确定的
16. millinery ['milinəri] *n.* 女帽
17. backer ['bækə] *n.* 赞助人，支援者
18. astute [əs'tju:t] *adj.* 精明的
19. publicist ['pʌblisist] *n.* 公关人员，宣传人员
20. jersey ['dʒə:zi] *n.* 针织运动衫
21. accessory [æk'sesəri] *n.* 配饰
22. casual ['kæʒjuəl] *adj.* 非正式的，休闲的

23. appropriate [ə'prəupriət] *adj.* 合适的，恰当的
24. corset ['kɔ:sit] *n.* 女士紧身内衣
25. loosely ['lu:sli] *adv.* 宽松地，松散地
26. garment ['gɑ:mənt] *n.* 服装，衣服
27. uncluttered ['ʌn'klʌtəd] *adj.* 整齐的，不凌乱的
28. ceaselessly ['si:slisli] *adv.* 不停地，持续地
29. wardrobe ['wɔ:drəub] *n.* 衣橱，衣柜；全部服装
30. masculine ['mɑ:skjulin] *adj.* 男性的，男子的
31. tailoring ['teilərɪŋ] *n.* 裁缝技术；成衣业
32. precise [pri'sais] *adj.* 精确的，准确的
33. individuality [,indi,vidju'æliti] *n.* 个性
34. riding breech 马裤
35. blazer ['bleizə] *n.* 运动衣，夹克
36. coordination [kəu'ɔ:di'neiʃən] *n.* 协调
37. cardigan ['kɑ:digən] *n.* 开襟羊毛衫
38. beige [beiʒ] *n.* 米色
39. palette ['pælit] *n.* 调色板
40. imitation [,imi'teiʃən] *adj.* 人造的，仿造的
41. gem [dʒem] *n.* 宝石
42. crystal ['kristl] *n.* 水晶
43. cluster ['klʌstə] *n.* 簇
44. string [strɪŋ] *n.* 一串；一行
45. perfume ['pə:fju:m] *n.* 香水，香料
46. couture [ku:'tuə] *n.* 女装（业）
47. relaunch [ri:'lɔ:ntʃ] *vt.* 重新发动，重新开办
48. braid [breid] *n.* 编织
49. crave [kreiv] *vt.* 渴望获得，迫切需要
50. ruthless ['ru:θlis] *adj.* 无情的，冷酷的，坚决的
51. emancipation [i,mænsi'peiʃən] *n.* 解放
52. tweak [twi:k] *vt.* 调整

Notes

「1」Time 100: The Most Important People of the Century：法国前文化部长曾经说过："从20世纪起，法国将有三个名字永留史册，那就是戴高乐、毕加索和香奈儿"，其实不只法国记住这些名字，世界也记住了这些名字。《时代周刊》在20世纪末评选的20世纪100个风云人物中，香奈儿作为唯一的服装设计师入选，因为她被认为不只影响了女性的

着装而且也影响了女性对自身的解放。

「2」Deauville：多维尔，法国海滨城市。

「3」Biarritz：比亚里茨，法国西南部一城市，位于西班牙边界附近的比斯开湾。

「4」Karl Lagerfeld：卡尔·拉格斐，出生于德国，后移居巴黎，著名的国际时装设计大师，担任香奈儿品牌的艺术总监，被称为"时装界的凯撒大帝""老佛爷"。

Exercises

Translate the following passage into Chinese.

All the famous innovations in fashion and design cannot outshine the fame of the single Chanel Little Black Dress. Coco Chanel introduced it in a time between the wars, when the bright colors and heavy embroideries dominated the fashion. The long-sleeved black dress, which was initially made for day in wool, and for evening in crepe, satin or velvet, shook up the world of fashion. Later appeared the other variations of a little black dress: short, sleeveless, in a pleated black chiffon, in black lace...

In 1926 American *Vogue* named Coco Chanel black dress 'a Ford', meaning it's simplicity and it's potential for an enormous and long-lasting success. The 'little black dress' is considered essential to a complete wardrobe by many women and fashion observers. It became a symbol of chic and sophisticated simplicity. Its ubiquity is such that it is often simply referred to as the 'LBD'.

Chanel LBD 1926

Chanel LBD 2008

Lesson 20 Hayao Miyazaki's Movie World

Miyazaki, the second of four brothers, was born in the town of Akebono-cho [1], part of Tokyo's Bunkyō-ku [2]. During World War II, Miyazaki's father Katsuji [3] was director of Miyazaki Airplane, owned by his brother (Hayao Miyazaki's uncle), which made rudders for A6M Zero fighter planes. During this time, Miyazaki drew airplanes and developed a lifelong fascination with aviation, a penchant that later manifested as a recurring theme in his films.

Hayao Miyazaki   *My Neighbor Totoro*

Miyazaki's mother was a voracious reader who often questioned socially accepted norms. Miyazaki later said that he inherited his questioning and skeptical mind from her. His mother underwent treatment for spinal tuberculosis from 1947 until 1955, and so the family moved frequently. Miyazaki's film *My Neighbor Totoro* [4] is set in that time period and features a family whose mother is in the hospital.

Miyazaki attended Toyotama High School. In his third year there, he saw the film *Hakujaden* [5], which has been described as 'the first-ever Japanese feature length color anime'. His interest in animation began in this period; however, in order to become an animator, he had to learn to draw the human figure, since his prior work had been limited to airplanes and battleships.

After high school, Miyazaki attended Gakushuin University [6], from which he would graduate in 1963 with degrees in political science and economics. He was a member of the 'Children's literature research club', the 'closest thing to a comics club in those days'.

In April 1963, Miyazaki got a job at Toei Animation [7], working as an in-between artist [8] on the anime *Wanwan Chushingura* [9]. He was a leader in a labor dispute soon after his arrival, becoming chief secretary of Toei's labor union in 1964.

Miyazaki first gained recognition while working as an in-between artist on the Toei production *Gulliver's Travels Beyond the Moon* [10]. He later played an important role as chief animator, concept artist, and scene designer on *Hols: Prince of the Sun* [11] in 1968, a landmark animated film directed by Isao Takahata [12], with whom he continued to collaborate for the next three decades.

Miyazaki left Toei in 1971 for A Pro, where he co-directed six episodes of the first *Lupin*

III [13] series with Isao Takahata. He and Takahata then began pre-production on a *Pippi Longstocking* series and drew extensive story boards for it. However, after traveling to Sweden to conduct research for the film and meet the original author, Astrid Lindgren [14], they were denied permission to complete the project, and it was canceled.

Miyazaki's next film, *Nausicaä of the Valley of the Wind* [15] was an adventure film that introduced many of the themes which recur in later films: a concern with ecology and the human impact on the environment; a fascination with aircraft and flight; pacifism. This was the first film both written and directed by Miyazaki. He adapted it from his manga series of the same title, which he began writing and illustrating two years earlier, but which remained incomplete until after the film's release.

Following the success of *Nausicaä of the Valley of the Wind*, Miyazaki co-founded the animation production company Studio Ghibli [16] with Takahata in 1985, and has produced nearly all of his subsequent work through it.

Nausicaä of the Valley of the Wind

Miyazaki continued to gain recognition with his next three films. *Laputa: Castle in the Sky* [17] (1986) recounts the adventure of two orphans seeking a magical castle-island that floats in the sky; *My Neighbor Totoro* [18] (Tonari no Totoro, 1988) tells of the adventure of two girls and their interaction with forest spirits; and *Kiki's Delivery Service* [19] (1989), adapted from a novel by Eiko Kadono [20], tells the story of a small-town girl who leaves home to begin life as a witch in a big city. Miyazaki's fascination with flight is evident throughout these films, ranging from the ornithopters flown by pirates in *Castle in the Sky*, to *the Totoro* and the Cat Bus soaring through the air, and Kiki flying her broom.

1997's *Princess Mononok* [21] returns to the ecological and political themes of *Nausicaä of the Valley of the Wind*. *Princess Mononoke* is also noted as one of his most violent pictures. The film was a huge commercial success in Japan, where it became the highest grossing film of all time, until the later success of *Titanic*, and it ultimately won Best Picture at the Japanese Academy Awards. Miyazaki went into what would prove to be temporary retirement after directing *Princess Mononoke* [22].

Princess Mononoke was the first Miyazaki film to use computer graphics. The demon snakes are computer-generated and composited onto Ashitaka, who is hand-drawn. Miyazaki has used traditional animation throughout the animation process, though computer-generated imagery was employed starting with *Princess Mononoke*. In an interview with *the Financial Times*, Miyazaki said 'it's very important for me to retain the right ratio between working by hand and computer. I have learnt that balance now, how to use both and still be able to call my films 2D'. Digital paint was also used for the first time in parts of *Princess Mononoke* in order to meet release deadlines. It was used as standard for subsequent films. However, in his 2008 film *Ponyo*[23], Miyazaki went back to traditional hand-drawn animation for everything, saying 'hand drawing on paper is the fundamental of animation'. Studio Ghibli's computer animation department was dissolved before production on *Ponyo* was started, and Miyazaki has decided to stick to hand drawn animation.

Laputa: Castle in the Sky   *Princess Mononoke*

Background Information

Hayao Miyazaki：宫崎骏，日本著名动画片导演，1941年1月5日生于东京。宫崎骏在全球动画界具有无可替代的地位，华特迪士尼称其为"动画界的黑泽明"。宫崎骏的每部作品，题材虽然不同，但却将梦想、环保、人生、生存这些令人反思的信息融合其中，是第一位将动画上升到人文高度的思想者，他这份执著，不仅令全球人产生共鸣，更受到全世界的重视。曾有人如此评价宫崎骏："夜空中可以没有月亮，但在动画界不能没有宫崎骏。"

Words and Expressions

1. rudder ['rʌdə] *n.* （船的）舵；（飞机的）方向舵
2. lifelong ['laif,lɔŋ] *adj.* 终身的，一辈子的
3. fascination [,fæsi'neiʃən] *n.* 迷恋，陶醉
4. penchant ['pentʃənt] *n.* 嗜好
5. voracious [və'reiʃəs] *adj.* 贪心的，贪婪的
6. skeptical ['skeptikəl] *adj.* 怀疑的
7. spinal ['spainl] *adj.* 脊柱的，脊骨的
8. animator ['æni,meitə] *n.* 动画片绘制者
9. comic ['kɔmik] *n.* 连环漫画

10. episode ['episəud] *n.* （电视等的）连续剧的一片段或一集
11. adventure [əd'ventʃə] *n.* 冒险
12. pacifism ['pæsifizəm] *n.* 和平主义
13. manga ['mæŋgə] *n.* 漫画
14. release [ri'li:s] *n.* 发行，发表
15. subsequent ['sʌbsikwənt] *adj.* 后来的，其后的
16. witch [witʃ] *n.* 女巫，巫婆
17. ornithopter [ˌɔ:ni'θɔptə] *n.* 扑翼飞机
18. pirate ['paiərit] *n.* 海盗
19. broom [bru:m] *n.* 扫帚
20. demon ['di:mən] *n.* 恶魔
21. composite ['kɔmpəzit] *adj.* 合成的，复合的
22. digital ['didʒitl] *adj.* 数字的，数位的

Notes

「1」Akebono-cho：曙町，位于东京都的立川市。

「2」Tokyo's Bunkyō-ku：东京文京区，位于东京二十三区中央。该区集中了日本不少的国、私立大、中、高等学校，因而有文化教育区的美名，日本最高学府——东京大学的本部校区即在该区。

「3」Katsuji：宫崎胜治。

「4」*My Neighbor Totoro*：动画电影《龙猫》，宫崎骏于1988年创作。

「5」*Hakujaden*：动画电影《白蛇传》，是一部由日本最大的动画制作公司——"东映动画"于1958年拍摄的动画电影，也是日本第一部彩色动画电影。

「6」Gakushuin University：学习院大学，由日本学校法人"学习院"设置、位于东京都丰岛区内的一所私立大学。

「7」Toei Animation：东映动画，成立于1948年，是日本老牌动画制作公司。很多有名的动画大师，如手冢治虫、宫崎骏、高畑勋等均是从东映动画出身。

「8」an in-between artist：中间画动画师，动画中的动作是由很多张画组成的，这些画的第一张跟最后一张被称为原画，其余中间的部分被称为中间画。

「9」*Wanwan Chushingura*：动画电影《汪汪忠臣藏》，1963年出版。

「10」*Gulliver's Travels Beyond the Moon*：动画电影《格列佛游记》。

「11」*Hols: Prince of the Sun*：动画电影《太阳王子》，全名为《太阳王子霍尔斯的大冒险》，1968年出版。

「12」Isao Takahata：高畑勋，日本著名动画电影导演、制作人，主要作品有《再见萤火虫》、《熊猫家族》、《隔壁的山田君》等。

「13」*Lupin III*：动画电影《鲁宾三世》，1971年出版。

「14」Astrid Lindgren：阿斯特里德·林德格伦 (1907—2002)，瑞典著名儿童文学女作家。

［15］*Nausicaä of the Valley of the Wind*：动画电影《风之谷》，吉卜力工作室推出的一部动画电影，该动画作品改编自宫崎骏连载于《Animage》的同名漫画。作品以假想中人类走向衰微的未来时代为背景，以主角娜乌西卡在战争中的各种探索为线索，内容涉及人与自然、理想社会、生命价值和意义等多方面问题，体现了作者对人类命运的严肃思考。

［16］*Studio Ghibli*：吉卜力工作室，工作室成立于1985年，由极富声望的导演宫崎骏及同事高畑勋、铃木敏夫等一起统筹，其细腻又富有生气、充满想象力的作品，在世界获得极高的评价。

［17］*Laputa: Castle in the Sky*：《天空之城》是日本吉卜力工作室于1986年推出的一部动画电影，《天空之城》的原作、监督、脚本和角色设定都是由宫崎骏来担任，使得这部作品从头到尾都充满了宫崎骏的理念。

［18］*My Neighbor Totoro*：《龙猫》这部影片充满了童话色彩和亲情的温馨，把观众成功地带入了一个梦幻般的童话世界里。Totoro同时也是吉卜力工作室的代言形象。

［19］*Kiki's Delivery Service*：《魔女宅急便》是日本童话作家角野荣子1985—2008年间写的5部小说的名字，其中第一部于1989年被吉卜力制作成动画电影。

［20］*Eiko Kadono*：角野荣子，日本著名儿童文学作家。1935年生于日本东京。毕业于日本早稻田大学。《女巫的特快专递》（即《魔女宅急便》）获日本野间儿童文学奖、小学馆文学奖。

［21］*Princess Mononok*：《幽灵公主》是吉卜力的第11部影片，这部由宫崎骏执导的电影应用了较多的计算机科技，这是吉卜力的一大挑战，为了应付这个挑战，吉卜力设立了一个专门的CG小组。

［22］在《幽灵公主》首映式上，宫崎骏宣布从此封笔。后来因为近藤喜文英年早逝，《我的邻居山田君》票房惨败，《泰坦尼克号》票房超过《幽灵公主》，激起宫崎骏的雄心万丈，撤回封笔宣言。1999再次正式返回吉卜力工作室，主持《千与千寻》的导演工作。

［23］*Ponyo*：《悬崖上的金鱼姬》。

Exercises

Read the following statements carefully, and decide whether they are true(T) or false(F) according to the passage.

1. Miyazaki's interest in animation was inspired when his father was director of Miyazaki Airplane.
2. Isao Takahata became Miyazaki's close associate in the next three decades since 1968.
3. *Pippi Longstocking* was the first film both written and directed by Miyazaki.
4. Many of the themes such as a concern with ecology and the human impact on the environment, a fascination with aircraft and flight, pacifism later manifested as recurring themes in his films.
5. Hayao Miyazaki's later works tended to use computer graphics.

Unit Four

Chinese Art

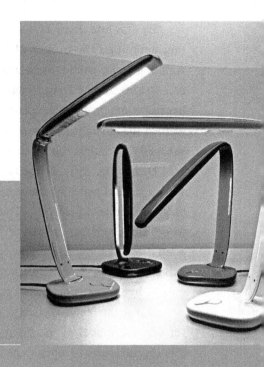

Lesson 21 Landscape Painting in Chinese Art

By the late Tang Dynasty, landscape painting had evolved into an independent genre that embodied the universal longing of cultivated men to escape their quotidian world to commune with nature. Such images might also convey specific social, philosophical, or political convictions. As the Tang Dynasty disintegrated, the concept of withdrawal into the natural world became a major thematic focus of poets and painters. Faced with the failure of the human order, learned men sought permanence within the natural world, retreating into the mountains to find a sanctuary from the chaos of dynastic collapse.

During the early Song Dynasty, visions of the natural hierarchy became metaphors for the well-regulated state. At the same time, images of the private retreat proliferated among a new class of scholar-officials [1]. These men extolled the virtues of self-cultivation—often in response to political setbacks or career disappointments—and asserted their identity as literati through poetry, calligraphy, and a new style of painting that employed calligraphic brushwork for self-expressive ends. The monochrome images of old trees, bamboo, rocks, and retirement retreats created by these scholar-artists became emblems of their character and spirit.

Durig the Yuan Dynasty, when many educated Chinese were barred from government service, the model of the Song literati retreat evolved into a full-blown alternative culture as this disenfranchised elite transformed their estates into sites for literary gatherings and other cultural pursuits [2]. These gatherings were frequently commemorated in paintings that, rather than presenting a realistic depiction of an actual place, conveyed the shared cultural ideals of a reclusive world through a symbolic shorthand in which a villa might be represented by a humble thatched hut. Because a man's studio or garden could be viewed as an extension of himself, paintings of such places often served to express the values of their owner.

During the Ming Dynasty, when native Chinese rule was restored, court artists produced conservative images that revived the Song metaphor for the state as a well-ordered imperial garden, while literati painters pursued self-expressive goals through the stylistic language of Yuan scholar-artists [3]. Shen Zhou (1427–1509) [4], the patriarch of the Wu school of painting centered in the cosmopolitan city of Suzhou, and his preeminent follower Wen Zhengming (1470–1559) [5] exemplified Ming literati ideals. Both men chose to reside at home rather than follow official careers, devoting themselves to self-cultivation through a lifetime spent reinterpreting the styles of Yuan scholar-painters.

Lesson 21 Landscape Painting in Chinese Art

Shen Zhou's portrait

Lofty Mount Lu, Shen Zhou

Wen Zhengming's portrait

Landscape painting, Wen Zhengming

  Morally charged images of reclusion remained a potent political symbol during the early years of the Qing Dynasty, a period in which many Ming loyalists lived in self-enforced retirement [6]. Often lacking access to important collections of old masters, loyalist artists drew inspiration from the natural beauty of the local scenery.

  Images of nature have remained a potent source of inspiration for artists down to the present day. While the Chinese landscape has been transformed by millennia of human occupation, Chinese artistic expression has also been deeply imprinted with images of the natural world. Viewing Chinese landscape paintings, it is clear that Chinese depictions of nature are seldom mere representations of the external world. Rather, they are expressions of the mind and heart of the individual artists–cultivated landscapes that embody the culture and cultivation of their masters.

Background Information

中国山水画简称"山水"。以山川自然景观为主要描绘对象的中国画，形成于魏晋南北朝时期，但尚未从人物画中完全分离。隋唐时始独立，五代、北宋时趋于成熟，成为中国画的重要画科。传统上按画法风格分为青绿山水、金碧山水、水墨山水、浅绛山水、小青绿山水、没骨山水等。

Words and Expressions

1. landscape ['lændskeip] n. 风景画，山水画
2. genre ['ʒɑ:nrə] n. （文学艺术等的）类型，流派
3. cultivated ['kʌltiveitid] adj. 文雅的；有教养的
4. quotidian [kwɔ'tidiən] adj. 平凡的
5. commune [kə'mju:n] vi. 与（大自然等）相交融
6. conviction [kən'vikʃən] n. 信念，信仰
7. withdrawal [wið'drɔ:əl] n. 退隐
8. thematic [θi'mætik] adj. 主题的
9. permanence ['pə:mənəns] n. 永久，永恒
10. sanctuary ['sæŋktjuəri] n. 庇护所，避难所
11. hierarchy ['haiərɑ:ki] n. 等级制度；层次体系
12. metaphor ['metəfə] n. 隐喻
13. proliferate [prə'lifəreit] vi. 激增
14. extoll [iks'tɔl] vt. 赞美，颂扬
15. virtue ['və:tju:] n. 美德，品德高尚
16. setback ['setbæk] n. 挫折，失败
17. literati [,litə'rɑ:ti:] n. 文人，学者
18. calligraphy [kə'ligrəfi] n. 书法
19. monochrome ['mɔnəkrəum] n. 单色，黑白
20. bar [bɑ:] vt. 禁止
21. full-blown ['ful'bləun] adj. 成熟的，完善的
22. alternative [ɔ:l'tə:nətiv] adj. 替代的
23. disenfranchised ['disin'fræntʃaiz] vt. 剥夺……的公民权
24. commemorate [kə'meməreit] vt. 纪念，庆祝，作为纪念物
25. thatched [θætʃt] adj. 茅草盖的
26. hut [hʌt] n. （简陋的）小屋
27. court [kɔ:t] n. 宫廷
28. conservative [kən'sə:vətiv] adj. 传统的，守旧的

29. patriarch ['peitriɑ:k] *n.* 创始人
30. cosmopolitan [ˌkɔzmə'pɔlitən] *adj.* 受各国文化影响的，世界性的，国际性的
31. reinterpret ['ri:in'tə:prit] *vt.* 重新解释
32. reclusion [ri'klu:ʒən] *n.* 隐居
33. Manchu [mæn'tʃu:] *n.* 满族人
34. loyalist ['lɔiəlist] *n.* 忠臣，效忠派
35. millennia [mi'leniə] *n.* (millennium的复数)千年期，千禧年

Notes

「1」scholar-officials：文人士大夫。中国绘画发展到宋、元之际，发生了一次明显变化，出现了较之唐代以来流行的精谨风格的绘画显得逸笔草草、不求形似的新画风，并且很快在文人士大夫中流行开来。这种画风即宋人康与之所谓"隐士之画"，亦称文人画，以别于民间画工和宫廷画院职业画家的绘画。文人画是一种象征的艺术，画家所创造的竹、梅、兰、菊、荷等已经完全不是自然物而是他自己内在生命的象征表现，讲求笔墨情趣，强调神韵，很重视文学、书法修养和画中意境的缔造。

「2」元代绘画是整个中国绘画史的分水岭，文人画开始成为画坛主流，是中国文人画发展的高峰时期。

「3」明代初年文人画家分为两派，一派忠于宋元文人画的传统，另一派是复古派，即明初复兴的皇家画院中继承南宋"马夏"院体山水画传统的戴进、吴伟等人。

「4」Shen Zhou：沈周（1427—1509），明代杰出书画家，字启南，号石田、白石翁、玉田生、有居竹居主人等。明代中期文人画"吴派"的开创者，与文徵明、唐寅、仇英并称"明四家"。传世作品有《庐山高图》《秋林话旧图》《沧州趣图》等。

「5」Wen Zhengming：文徵明（1470—1559），明代中期著名的画家、书法家，号"衡山居士"，世称"文衡山"。传世画作有《千岩竞秀》《万壑争流》《湘君夫人图》《石湖草堂》等。

「6」清代是文人画鼎盛的时期，涌现了诸多顶极文人画家，最突出的是"四僧"，身为明末遗民，对反抗无望的现实作消极的反抗，在书画中寄寓国破家亡之痛。四人都擅长山水画，各有风格。他们都极力发挥其创造性，反对摹古，直抒胸臆，取得创新成就。

Exercises

Translate the following passage into Chinese.

To disguise his identity, Zhu Da, a scion of the Ming imperial family, took refuge in a Buddhist temple after the Manchu conquest of 1644. About 1680, he renounced his status as a monk and began producing paintings and calligraphy in order to support himself. In 1684, he took the biehao (artistic name) Bada Shanren. A staunch Ming loyalist throughout his life, Bada used painting as a means of protest. This painting is typical of the bold, enigmatic images that Bada produced during the last twenty years of his life. Treating the image as a calligraphic design, Bada juxtaposes large and small, solid and void, and heavy and light, creating a tension between flat shapes and three-dimensional volumes that heightens the disturbing quality.

Fish and Rocks

Lesson 22 Chinese Folk Art

Chinese folk art is an important part of the country's extremely rich cultural and art heritage. Chinese folk art has won recognition and praise from experts both at home and abroad for its great variety, sincere rural content, rich flavor of life, distinctive local style, and its artistic approaches of romanticism.

The folk artist is at his best in understanding and depicting life in its wholeness, and apt to show its rhythms and melodies. He relies on his intuition, impressions and memories, as well as his experience and understanding of life to grasp the essence of the phenomena or objects he depicts, thus making the artistic images quite different from their original models. In artistic representation and expression, works of folk art are straightforward, natural, flexible, vivid and intimate. They reside, in roundabout ways, ideas in particular images, reason in emotion, and feelings in concrete forms. Ingenuity is found in simplicity, exquisiteness in crudeness, and humor in clumsiness. Folk artists also use decorative, figurative, allegoric and symbolic methods with magical deftness. Since ancient times, Chinese folk art has been seeking to understand and present the lofty spirit of the Chinese nation. It has given expression to the indomitable morale and character of the Chinese people shown in their constant efforts to open up new paths for development.

Like a galaxy of brilliant gems, folk art embraces all aspects of daily life and is loved by the masses. The materials that most commonly used are the ordinary natural substances that come readily to hand. Folk artists are familiar with the aesthetic habits of the people, and their feel of life is based on the aesthetic experiences of the masses. In creating art forms, they are guided by their mind, reason and aesthetic rules. Some of their works seem to be crudely made, but they show great ingenuity, originality, simplicity and purity, which implies a profound philosophy of art. Works of folk art afford people not only aesthetic enjoyment and amusement, but also knowledge and education. Folk artists have been under the edifying influence of folk art since their early childhood, and a seed of beauty was planted in their hearts when they became apprentices to elder folk artists. Their love for the beautiful is eternal.

Folk shadow play

Folk New Year painting

Folk embroidery

Folk toy

Crafts, the largest category of folk art, perfectly combines the material and spiritual life of the people because they have both utilitarian and aesthetic value. Folk art is born of heart. It is not something that has become rigidly fixed; instead, it steadily develops as it tries to meet people's need for appreciation of the beautiful. As a form of the traditional Chinese art, folk art is an intermixture of the aesthetic psychology of society and the aesthetic psychology of the artists, which externalizes itself through palpable media. It will develop with history, society and people's life.

Shaanxi folk art

The middle reaches of Yellow River are the cradle of Chinese culture. The ancestors of the Chinese people have lived and multiplied the earth here since the primitive age. In Chinese history, Shaanxi had for a very long time been the political center of the country and boasted the nation's most developed culture and art. Xi'an was the capital of the Western Zhou, Qin, Western Han, Sui, Tang and six other dynasties, covering a period of more than 1 120 years. The famous Silk Road started and ran westward from the city, which has long economic and cultural contacts with Japan and Korea and, through the Silk Road, with India, Indo-China[1], Middle Asia, West Asia and some European countries and regions. It was once the cultural center of the East.

Ancient artifacts found in the province include the unsophisticated, beautiful Banpo painted pottery[2] and Tang figurines; the majestic and firm bronzeware of Zhou Dynasty; the bricks of the Qin Dynasty; the tiles of the Han Dynasty; the stone tablets bearing engraved images of the Han Dynasty; the Terra-Cotta Warriors and Soldiers of the Qin Dynasty; and the stone cavings and murals of the Han and Tang Dynasties. All of them are classic examples of Chinese arts, crystallizing in them the wisdom and skill of the artisans of the past.

Lesson 22 Chinese Folk Art

A wide range of Shaanxi folk arts, among them, the paper cutting is one of the most representative folk art in Shaanxi. Shaanxi paper-cuts have a long history. Originating in the cradle of ancient Chinese culture, they have been handed down from generation to generation among people. Folk paper-cut, though often used as patterns for embroidery, serve as window decorations. When Spring Festival comes, the windows of the houses on the Guanzhong Plain and of the caves on the Northern Shaanxi Plateau are decorated with papercuts. With bright red paper-cuts of all kinds on snow-white window paper, the atmosphere appears a lot more festive. At the same time, the paper-cuts contain people's good wishes.

The subjects of Shaanxi paper-cuts are considered to be both bold and unconstrained, brief and exaggerated works of art. Different parts of the province have styles of their own. The Northern Shaanxi paper-cuts look comparatively simple, honest and vigorous, while the Central Shaanxi Plain's paper-cuts are of simplicity, mingled with exquisiteness. They seem to tell us vividly of the ancient stories of the Chinese nation and pull at the heartstring of the Chinese people.

The Northern Shaanxi paper-cuts   The Central Shaanxi Plain's paper-cuts

Background Information

Chinese Folk Art：中国民间艺术是中国人民群众创作的，以美化环境、丰富民间风俗活动为目的的日常生活中的实用艺术。

民间艺术是组成各民族艺术传统的重要因素，为一切艺术形式的源泉。新石器时代的彩陶艺术，中国战国秦汉的石雕、陶俑、画像砖石，其造型、风格均具鲜明的民间艺术特色。

民间艺术与民俗活动关系极为密切，如民间的节日庆典、婚丧嫁娶、生子祝寿、迎神赛会等活动中的年画、剪纸、春联、道具、花灯、扎纸、符道神像、服装饰件、龙舟彩船、月饼花模、泥塑等及少数民族民俗节日中的服饰、布置等。

民间艺术分布于各地，因地域、风俗、感情、气质的差异又形成丰富的品类和风格，但它们都具有实用价值与审美价值统一的特点。另外，它们的制作材料大都是普通的木、布、纸、竹、泥土，但制作技巧高超、构思巧妙，擅长大胆想象、夸张，且常用人们熟悉

的寓意谐音手法，积极乐观、清新刚健、淳朴活泼，表达了对美好生活的憧憬与理想，富有浪漫主义色彩。

Words and Expressions

1. variety [vəˈraiəti] n. 种类；多样化
2. sincere [sinˈsiə] adj. 真挚的，真诚的
3. at his best 处于最好状态，处于全盛时期
4. rhythm [ˈriðəm] n. 节奏，韵律
5. melody [ˈmelədi] n. 旋律
6. intuition [ˌintjuːˈiʃən] n. 直觉
7. grasp [grɑːsp] vt. 抓住；理解，领会
8. straightforward [streitˈfɔːwəd] adj. 率真的，坦率的
9. flexible [ˈfleksəbl] adj. 灵活的，变通的
10. vivid [ˈvivid] adj. 生动的
11. intimate [ˈintimit] adj. 亲密的，熟悉的
12. reside [riˈzaid] vi. 存在
13. roundabout [ˈraundəbaut] adj. 绕道的；不直截了当的
14. concrete [ˈkɔnkriːt] adj. 具体的，具象的
15. ingenuity [ˌindʒiˈnjuːiti] n. 机智，巧妙，精巧
16. exquisiteness [ˈekskwizitnis] n. 优美，精致
17. figurative [ˈfigjurətiv] adj. 比喻的
18. allegoric [ˌæleˈgɔrik] adj. 寓言的
19. deftness [ˈdeftnis] n. 熟练，灵巧
20. indomitable [inˈdɔmitəbl] adj. 坚强不屈的
21. morale [məˈraːl] n. 士气，斗志
22. galaxy [ˈgæləksi] n. 一群（尤指出色的人或灿烂的事物）
23. gem [dʒem] n. 宝石；宝物，珍品
24. substance [ˈsʌbstəns] n. 物质
25. afford [əˈfɔːd] vt. 提供，给予
26. amusement [əˈmjuːzmənt] n. 娱乐，消遣
27. edifying [ˈedifaiiŋ] adj. 有教化意味的
28. apprentice [əˈprentis] n. 学徒，徒弟
29. eternal [iˈtəːnəl] adj. 永恒的，永久的
30. category [ˈkætigəri] n. 种类
31. utilitarian [ˌjuːtiliˈtɛəriən] adj. 实用的

32. intermixture [ˌintə'mikstʃə] *n.* 混合
33. externalize [eks'tə:nəlaiz] *vt.* 赋予外形，使具体化
34. palpable ['pælpəbl] *adj.* 可感知的，可摸到的
35. cradle ['kreidl] *n.* 摇篮；发源地
36. boast [bəust] *vt.* 以有……而自豪
37. unsophisticated ['ʌnsə'fistikeitid] *adj.* 纯真的
38. majestic [mə'dʒestik] *adj.* 雄伟的，威严的
39. tablet ['tæblit] *n.* （铭刻文字的）匾、碑
40. engrave [in'greiv] *vt.* 雕刻
41. terra-cotta [ˌterə'kɔtə] *n.* 陶俑
42. mural ['mjuərəl] *n.* 壁画
43. crystallizing ['kristəlaiziŋ] *n.* 结晶
44. bold [bəuld] *adj.* 大胆的，无畏的
45. unconstrained [ˌʌnkən'streind] *adj.* 不受约束的

Notes

「1」Indo-China:中南半岛,因为新航路开辟之后,欧洲人普遍认为亚洲只有两个国家,即中国和印度,所以对于印度和中国的"接合部"称 中南半岛。

「2」Banpo painted pottery:半坡彩陶,距今有七千年的历史,是中国彩陶文化历史较早、特点突出、影响较大的一个类型。

Exercises

Read the following statements carefully, and decide whether they are true(T) or false(F) according to the text.

1. The folk artist understand life so deep that the artistic images they created are very close to their original models.

2. Folk art plays the roles of understanding, education, application and aesthetics.

3. Chinese folk art, which is of very distinctive national features, carries abundant spiritual implications and reveals laboring people's ways of thinking, their concepts of value and aesthetic delights.

4. The Central Shaanxi Plain's paper-cuts look comparatively simple, honest and vigorous, while Northern Shaanxi paper-cuts are of simplicity, mingled with exquisiteness.

Lesson 23　Eric Chan—Finding Balance in Design

'More technology is not the right answer, but the right technology can help us find the answer.'

—Eric Chan

For more than 25 years, Eric Chan has been asking many tough questions. Forever considered the consummate designer, Chan spends much of his time pondering about humans and their behavior, trends, materials, and how these can be balanced to attain better design. His priority in thinking transcends fashion and aesthetics and rather examines how functions can be implemented to better compliment and enhance usage for a given product, service, or even an entire system (like public transport).

Eric Chan

Steadfast to his role as an industrial designer, Chan remains determined to know how different individuals would use and react to a design. As a designer, he is constantly thinking about how we can ensure that the tools and knowledge we use adequately keeps pace with constant, rapid change.

Through his own New York-based practise ECCO Design, established in 1989, Chan has helped a growing list of international clients improve what they do through principles of user-centric design. Fundamental to his tenet is the idea that designers should be intelligently responsible for mediating balance between people and products, business and community, technology and nature — and ultimately bring transformation to society.

Born in Guangzhou, Chan was raised and educated in Hong Kong, where he graduated from Hong Kong Polytechnic University[1] in 1976 with a degree in Industrial design. He then traveled to the US to study at Cranbrook Academy of Art[2], a school at the forefront of American design. Through the scholastic experience Chan was able to learn from and work with pioneers in the fields of product and ergonomic design, which has significantly influenced his professional practise and methodology. As practising inventor, Chan's obsessions with life-enriching innovation has manifested in many contemplative efforts, earning him a number of patents.

His consultancy, ECCO, is an established and widely revered firm best known for success in addressing the needs of multinational companies in every major consumer segment including Herman Miller[3], Virgin[4], Toyota[5], KEF[6], LG Electronics[7] and Lenovo[8]. With creations bounded only by the limits of his own imagination, Chan, who often incorporates groundbreaking—in one form or another —new ideas to his subjects, has designed more than a dozen bestselling chairs, mobile phones, CD players, washing machines, a stapler, office furniture, in-vehicle interactive voice-command systems, refrigerators, headphones and numerous others. Of particular note has been his holistic work to re-imagine public transportation for New Jersey Transport's multi-level railcar.

Ribbon lamp

Orca mini stapler

The design philosophy behind ECCO looks beyond being style driven and iconic, to pursue opportunities that incorporate elements of social responsibility, ecological sensitivity, and cultural connectivity. It synergizes usability needs, innovation, insightful creativity, break-through engineering, and poetic interpretation in order to design meaningful products and experiences.

Although pragmatic in his demeanor — upholding design as a tool of business and society—Chan's work has nonetheless been featured in numerous international publications, as well as in the permanent collections of museums worldwide. These include: the London Design Museum, Musee des Arts Decoratifs de Montreal[9], the Israel Museum, the Museum Die Neue Sammlung[10] in Germany and the Museum of Modern Art in New York.

ID magazine named Chan as one of the 40 most influential designers in the US, while *Business Week* hailed him 'one of the new breed of ingenious American designers that is making the world take note'. Contract magazine conferred similar commendation in 2007 when he was listed amongst the ten most influential designers in the United States. In 2009, he was recognised for his achievement in designing the groundbreaking a Modular Hardware/ Software Mobile Device for Bug Labs[11] with a 2009 World Technology Award in Entertainment, edging out some world-renowned finalists from video-gaming, academia, and television.

An active member of IDSA, Chan's commitment to the design community includes serving as juror for Industrial Design Excellence Awards and CES Awards[12] for Industrial Design.

In recent years, he has focused his concerns on expanding the contemporary vocabulary of Chinese design. In 2007, Chan teamed up with Herman Miller to research and design a modern, ergonomically-sound armchair made from bamboo.Combining traditional craft with computerised techniques, the groundbreaking chair stirred Chan's desire to probe further the means to heighten design from his native heritage, which now forms a crucial part of Chan's strategies. He received the World's Outstanding Chinese Designer (WOCD) award at the Hong Kong Design Centre (HKDC) on December 3, 2010.

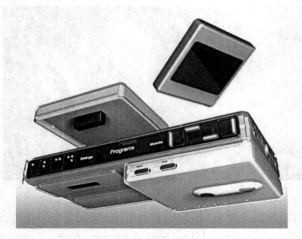

ECCO bug flying modules

Eric Chan's ECCO 9707 bamboo chair

Background Information

Eric Chan：陈秉鹏，著名的产品设计师，其作品获多份国际级刊物刊载，并已成为世界各地博物馆的珍藏。于2007年被Contract杂志列为美国十大最具影响力的设计师之一，更被*Business Week*誉为"举世瞩目的美国新一代天才设计师"。

1989年在纽约创立自己的设计公司ECCO Design，与不同商业机构合作，设计多类型产品，包括日用品、家具、家庭电器、公共轨道交通、滑翔飞机等。陈秉鹏认为成功的产品设计不只是美观的，还要实用、对环境不造成损害，而且能赚钱。因此，ECCO设计团队的工作便包括了各式各样的研究，如人类工程学、市场调查、对人类行为、生活习惯进行观察、物料研究、新科技的发展等。

Words and Expressions

1. consummate ['kən'sʌmit]   *adj.* 技艺高超的，熟练的
2. ponder ['pɔndə]   *vi.* 仔细考虑
3. transcend [træn'send]   *vt.* 超越，优于
4. implement ['impliment]   *vt.* 实施，执行

5. compliment ['kɔmplimənt] *vt.* 恭维；赞美
6. steadfast ['stedfəst] *adj.* 坚定的，不动摇的
7. keep pace with 跟上，与……并驾齐驱
8. tenet ['tenit] *n.* 宗旨，原则
9. mediate ['mi:dieit] *vt.* 调停，调解
10. forefront ['fɔ:frʌnt] *n.* 最前列，最前方
11. obsession [əb'seʃən] *n.* 着迷
12. consultancy [kən'sʌltənsi] *n.* 咨询公司，顾问公司
13. revere [ri'viə] *vt.* 尊敬，崇敬
14. address [ə'dres] *vt.* 对付；满足
15. multinational [ˌmʌlti'næʃənl] *adj.* 跨国公司的
16. groundbreaking ['graund,breikiŋ] *adj.* 开创性的
17. dozen ['dʌzn] *n.* 一打；许多
18. stapler ['steiplə] *n.* 订书机
19. holistic [həu'listik] *adj.* 全部的，整体的
20. railcar ['reil,kɑ:] *n.* 轨道车
21. synergize ['sinədʒaiz] *vt.* 协同，加强
22. pragmatic [præg'mætik] *adj.* 实际的，实干的
23. demeanor [di'mi:nə] *n.* 举止，行为
24. hail [heil] *vt.* 承认……为，拥立
25. modular ['mɔdjulə] *adj.* 组装的，组合的
26. edging out 替代
27. juror ['dʒuərə] *n.* 评委
28. stir [stə:] *vt.* 唤起；激起
29. probe [prəub] *vt.* 探索
30. prelude ['prelju:d] *n.* 开端；序幕；前奏

Notes

「1」Hong Kong Polytechnic University：香港理工大学，成立于1937年，为全港学生人数最多的大学教育资助委员会（University Grants Committee）资助的大学。

「2」Cranbrook Academy of Art：克兰布鲁克艺术学院，创建于1932年，是由美国报业巨头乔治·布什和来自芬兰的建筑大师埃利·沙里宁共同创办的，位于美知名汽车城底特律的僻静郊外。克兰布鲁克艺术学院是全世界顶级的以研究生教育为主的一流艺术设计学院，开创了具有美国风格的新工业设计体系，被称为"现代美国设计师的摇篮"。

「3」Herman Miller：赫曼米勒，美国最大的办公家具生产商。

「4」Virgin：维珍集团，是英国多家使用维珍作为品牌名称的企业所组成的集团，由著名的英国商人理查德·布兰森爵士创办。集团业务范围包括旅游、航空、电器、娱乐业等。

「5」Toyota：丰田，日本著名汽车工业公司。

「6」KEF：全称为Kent Engineering Fonndy，英国音响器材公司。

「7」LG Electronics：LG电子，隶属于韩国著名企业LG集团，集团覆盖化学能源、电机电子、机械金属、贸易服务、金融及公益事业、体育六大领域，而LG电子是LG集团最大的子公司。

「8」Lenovo：联想，中国著名的国际化科技公司，由联想及原IBM个人计算机事业部所组成。

「9」Musee des Arts Decoratifs de Montreal：蒙特利尔装饰艺术博物馆。

「10」Museum Die Neue Sammlung：慕尼黑国际设计博物馆。

「11」Bug Labs：美国纽约一家专营手持式电子设备的公司。

「12」CES Awards：全称为Consumer Electronics Show Awards，国际消费电子展奖。

Exercises

Translate the following passage into Chinese.

Created in partnership with Herman Miller, ECCO 9707 utilizes individually flexing bamboo slats in its seat and back to provide comfort and ergonomic support. Held in place by three horizontal polymer strips — two across the back and one across the seat — the reeds function like springs, bowing and cradling the body when pressed against, and bouncing back to their original place when pressure is let up. Only 15 of the chairs exist, unfortunately, as they were made for a special exhibit at the Hong Kong Design Centre. However, Chan is continuing to experiment with the material and the technology, hoping to apply it to a mass-produced product.

Unit Five

Design Education

Lesson 24 Birmingham Institute of Art and Design

The Birmingham Institute of Art and Design (officially abbreviated as BIAD) is the largest British university art and design teaching and research centre outside London. It is a faculty of Birmingham City University[1] and the largest, most successful department of the university. *The Sunday Times University Guide 2004*[2] stated, 'Rated excellent Art and Design'. Birmingham City University states that 'BIAD received an excellent Quality Assurance score of 22/24 for Art and Design' from the QAA[3].

The Birmingham Institute of Art and Design

BIAD dates back, in various incarnations, to the year 1843. It reached its full maturity from the 1890s, as the Birmingham Municipal School of Art at Margaret Street, under the leadership of Edward R. Taylor. The Birmingham School led the way in introducing executed design to the teaching of art and design nationally (working in the material for which the design was intended rather than designing on paper). A specialised branch school, the School of Jewellery, opened in 1890 in Birmingham's Jewellery Quarter. By September 1893, when the extension to the central school building opened, staff appointments had been made in the fields of embroidery, needlework and wood-engraving, and a number of 'art laboratories' or workshops for practical instruction in fresco, modelling and woodwork had been created. In 1901 the School Committee suggested further extending the syllabus to include stained glass, bookbinding, and writing (illumination and calligraphy).

The main BIAD campus and library is located at Gosta Green, just north of Birmingham city centre. It is adjacent to Aston University. There are also smaller centres located in: Bournville (Centre for Visual Arts, foundation awards and evening classes) in the suburbs south of the city centre; Margaret Street (Fine Art) in the city centre next to Birmingham Central Library and Birmingham Museum & Art Gallery; and Vittoria Street (School of Jewellery) in the city's Jewellery Quarter. The International Project Space at Bournville hosts international art exhibitions and residencies. BIAD at Gosta Green is home to User-lab, a research and design laboratory specialising in user-centred design.

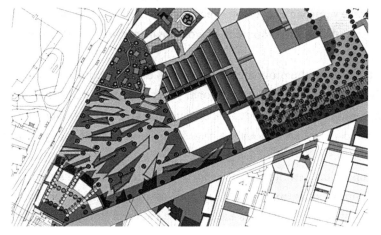

BIAD landscape artchitecture design   BIAD fashion design

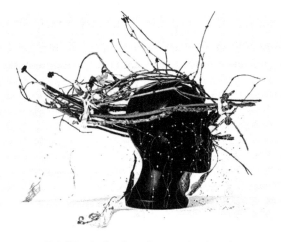

BIAD visual communication design   BA (Hons) visual arts by negotiated study

Five Schools deliver a wide range of further and higher education courses and a programme of research: School of Art, School of Jewellery, School of Architecture, School of Fashion, Textiles, Three-Dimensional Design and School of Visual Communication.

The School of Jewellery is the largest institution in Europe for provision of education and training in the fields of jewellery and related subjects. Its courses span a wide range of types and levels of experience: from introductory classes for secondary schools right up to Ph.D. research degrees.

BA (Hons) jewellery and silversmithing

The course has grown and developed to be one of the most highly respected in the country. One of its strengths is its diverse approach to the subject—there is no 'house style'. Your individuality is encouraged through the development of your own personal philosophy and direction.

The structure of projects throughout the programme encourages the development of practical making skills alongside creative thinking. The use of traditional skills and processes with precious metals is balanced with the exploration of non-precious metals and unconventional materials. This allows fine jewellery making to co-exist harmoniously alongside fashion and catwalk jewellery, functional tableware and accessories.

External projects and competitions are important aspects of the course. Links with other subject areas in BIAD are encouraged as appropriate, as well as opportunities for overseas collaboration and exchange. Recent student successes have included several European prizes and exhibitions.

Graduates from the programme go on to a diverse range of careers, including designers for the jewellery and silver industry; designer/ makers; artist/ jewellers, consultants and administrators. A significant number progress every year to Master's and Research courses. Postgraduate courses are essential for those pursuing a teaching career.

BIAD jewellery and silversmithing design

BIAD jewellery and silversmithing design

Background Information

Birmingham Institute of Art and Design：伯明翰艺术设计学院成立于1843年，是英国最大最知名的专业艺术设计学院之一，也是伯明翰城市大学（前中央英格兰大学）的一部分。学院开设专业齐全的预科、专科、本科、研究生和博士的课程。2005年学院被《卫报》评为全英十佳专业艺术设计学院。

伯明翰艺术设计学院拥有视觉传达系、媒体系、产品造型系、纯艺术系、服装设计系、织物系和珠宝设计系等六大科系,它们分布在伯明翰市内五个不同的校区。每一个分系都拥有自己强大的专业师资阵容和绝对高品质的硬件设施,特别是珠宝学院享有"欧洲第一"的美誉。许多毕业生已经成为世界级的设计师,并在国际设计比赛中获奖。

Words and Expressions

1. faculty ['fækəlti] *n.* (大学的)系,院
2. incarnation [,inkɑː'neiʃən] *n.* 化身
3. maturity [mə'tjuəriti] *n.* 成熟,完善
4. lead the way 引领,带路
5. quarter ['kwɔːtə] *n.* (城市中的)区
6. extension [iks'tenʃən] *n.* 扩大部分
7. fresco ['freskəu] *n.* 壁画;湿壁画
8. syllabus ['siləbəs] *n.* 教学大纲
9. bookbinding ['buk,baindiŋ] *n.* 装订术
10. adjacent [ə'dʒeisnt] *adj.* 毗邻的
11. residency ['rezidənsi] *n.* (乐团等)常驻演出;(医科毕业生)住院实习(期)
12. unconventional ['ʌnkən'venʃənl] *adj.* 非常规的
13. alongside [ə'lɔŋ'said] *adv.* 并排地
14. tableware ['teiblwɛə] *n.* 餐具

Notes

「1」Birmingham City University:伯明翰城市大学,是英国最大的现代化、综合性的高等学府之一,其历史最早可追溯到1843年。其下属学院包括:伯明翰艺术设计学院;商学院(包括计算机系);伯明翰音乐学院;教育学院;技术创新中心;法律、人文、发展和社会学院;教育学院;健康和公共卫生学院。大学提供语言、预科、本科、硕士及博士层次的教育,专业设置广泛,涵盖了管理、建筑、艺术、环境科学、计算机、工程、教育、法律、社会科学及音乐领域。

「2」*The Sunday Times University Guide 2004*:《星期天泰晤士报》"2004年大学指南",该指南自2000年开始一直持续至今年。通过对英国各高校专业的综合比较,以及英国各大学不同专业的就业和起薪情况的介绍,帮助学生选择大学。该指南具有相当的影响力。

「3」QAA:全英高等教育质量保证委员会(Quality Assurance Agency)是英国最具权威的教育质量评估的政府机构。该机构每年都要对全英上百所高校做严格审核,审核结果是对高校教育质量的权威评价。

Exercises

Translate the following passage into Chinese.

Accommodation

The University offers accommodation in Halls of Residence at various locations throughout Birmingham. All Halls are offered at a minimum forty-week contract. In addition, the University can provide details of accommodation in the private sector. For students with special needs we have accessible purpose-built units at some of the Halls of Residence, and further information is available on request. The range of accommodation offered includes catered, en-suite, and units suitable for postgraduates and for students with small families.

It is not possible to guarantee a room at your preferred residence, and priority for on-campus accommodation is normally given to students whose courses are based on the campus in question. Full-time students who live within the greater Birmingham area may similarly receive an offer of accommodation, if sufficient rooms are available.

Once you have received your offer of a place, you will be sent an accommodation pack which gives more detailed information about accommodation and will include an application form to be completed and returned. Most offers of accommodation are made over the summer period after any outstanding examination results are confirmed.

Lesson 25 Savannah College of Art and Design

The Savannah College of Art and Design was founded in 1978 to provide college degree programs not previously available in southeast Georgia and to create a specialized professional art college to attract students from throughout the United States and abroad. In 1979, SCAD opened its doors with five trustees, four staff members, seven faculty member, and 71 students. At that time the school offered eight majors. The curriculum was established with dual goals of excellent arts education and effective career preparation for students. Today, with multiple locations and online distance education offerings, SCAD continues to assiduously adhere to these goals.

SCAD.

SAVANNAH COLLEGE of ART and DESIGN

SCAD logo

In the spring of 1979, SCAD purchased and renovated the Savannah Volunteer Guard Armory to serve as the first classroom and administration building. The historic significance of the 1892 structure was recognized by its nomination for inclusion in the National Register of Historic Places. Named Poetter Hall in honor of two of the founders, the building remains in active use by SCAD today.

SCAD exists to prepare talented students for professional careers, emphasizing learning through individual attention in a positively oriented university environment. The goal of the university is to nurture and cultivate the unique qualities of each student through an interesting curriculum, in an inspiring environment, under the leadership of involved professors.

SCAD Poetter Hall

SCAD-eLearning

SCAD is a private, nonprofit institution accredited by the Commission on Colleges of the Southern Association of Colleges and Schools [1] to award bachelor's and master's degrees. The university confers Bachelor of Arts, Bachelor of Fine Arts, Master of Architecture, Master of Arts, Master of Arts in Teaching, Master of Fine Arts and Master of Urban Design degrees, as well as undergraduate and graduate certificates. The professional M.Arch. degree is accredited by the National Architectural Accrediting Board. The Master of Arts in Teaching degrees offered by SCAD are approved by the Georgia Professional Standards Commission. The SCAD interior design Bachelor of Fine Arts degree is accredited by the Council for Interior Design Accreditation. SCAD is licensed by the South Carolina Commission on Higher Education.

Class size is small, allowing each student the opportunity to receive individual attention. Faculty members have distinguished backgrounds in their fields. The international faculty and student body come from all 50 states and 100 countries. An English as a Second Language program and dedicated international student services staff are available to assist international students with the adjustment to university life in the United States.

Aimation class

Advertising class

SCAD values:

Providing an exceptional education and life-changing experience for students.

Demonstrating quality and excellence in every aspect of operations.
Sustaining a respectful and honest university environment.
Growing while continually improving.
Being innovative and results-oriented.
Promoting a cooperative team spirit and a positive 'can-do' attitude.
Going the 'extra mile'.
SCAD offers an array of degrees and programs through the following academic divisions:
School of Building Arts
School of Communication Arts
School of Design
School of Film, Digital Media and Performing Arts School of Fine Arts
School of Foundation Studies
School of Liberal Arts
SCAD-eLearning animation class

Background Information

Savannah College of Art and Design：萨凡纳艺术设计学院，位于美国东南部的佐治亚州的萨凡纳市，是美国最大的私立艺术学院和美国东南部重要的艺术学院之一。学院的学术水平在美国艺术教育领域口碑很佳。1991年，美国国家建筑教育评估委员会（NAAB）鉴定并认可了萨凡纳艺术设计学院的建筑学专业提供的五年建筑专业硕士课程。这是在美国艺术学院中为数不多的在短期内取得如此学术地位的艺术教育机构。萨凡纳艺术设计学院的国际背景也很强，在欧洲、亚洲的学术活动频繁。有资格授予美术学士、建筑硕士、艺术硕士及美术硕士等学位。艺术学院课程设置的目标有两个：提供优秀的艺术教育和实用的职前准备。

Words and Expressions

1. trustee [trʌs'ti:] n. （公司、学校等的）理事，董事
2. dual ['dju:əl] adj. 双倍的；双重的
3. offering ['ɔ:fəriŋ] n. 课程
4. renovate ['renouveit] vt. 修理；改善；翻新

Notes

「1」the Southern Association of Colleges and Schools：美国南部院校联盟，简称为SACS，是美国最具权威的六大联盟认证机构之一。美国以区域划分，基本上分成六大地区的质量认证委员会，也是美国院校主流质量认证机构。

Exercises

Translate the following passage into Chinese.

As the University for Creative Careers, SCAD is dedicated to helping students and alumni succeed in their chosen fields. The office of career and alumni success helps you find internships, provides you with job-search assistance, and offers extensive resources to match you with your dream job.

If you want individualized guidance about course selection or help with resumes, portfolios, interviews and other job-search strategies, career advisers will assist you. Career and alumni success also offers workshops and classes about entrepreneurship, branding, salary negotiation, socially responsible careers and more. Last year, more than 175 companies and organizations visited SCAD to meet and recruit our students and alumni. These companies conducted job interviews, reviewed portfolios, delivered presentations and participated in faculty/ student networking events.

参考答案

Lesson 1　Arts and Crafts Movement

　　1. B　2. C　3. C　4. A

Lesson 2　Art Nouveau

　　1. T　2. F　3. T　4. F　5. T

Lesson 3　Constructivism

　　构成主义运动起源于俄国，是从1919年开始的一场艺术和建筑运动，该运动反对"为艺术而艺术"的观念，支持将艺术作为一种实践导向的社会目的。作为一个积极的力量，构成主义一直持续到1934年左右，在被社会主义写实主义取代之前，它对魏玛共和国和其他地方的艺术的发展具有重要影响。其主题在以后其他的艺术运动中偶有出现。

Lesson 4　Bauhaus and the Education of Design

　　1. F　2. F　3. T　4. F　5. T　6. F

Lesson 5　The International Typographic Style

　　国际主义平面设计风格的特征是：利用模数化的网格提供一个统一有序的结构；无衬线字体（特别是1961年推出的赫尔维提加体）左边对齐，右边则参差不齐；黑白摄影图片取代手绘插图。总体印象是简洁理性、结构紧密、明确客观以及浑然一体。

Lesson 6　Corporate Identity

　　略。

Lesson 7　Book Designer Fiona Raven

　　封面是书的前部，为了使书籍脱颖而出，封面通常至少包含书名和作者，也许还有适当的插图。封面内一直延伸到左页的是前环衬页，有时是欧洲出版商联合会的出版规定内容，而环衬页另一半自由的页面被称为扉页。传统上，手工装订的书籍中，环衬页只是一张空白纸或装饰纸，隐蔽地加强了封面和书芯之间的连接。在现代书籍中，例如，在纯文本书籍中它可以是空白页，而在如儿童读物和咖啡桌上的摆放书等类型的书籍中，装饰丰富，插图设计得更为大胆。

　　书脊是一本书的垂直边缘，因为它通常立在书架上，按照惯例，上面印有文字信息。在美国出版或印刷的文本中，当书籍垂直摆放时，书脊的文本是从上到下排列，即当书籍封面朝上平放时，书脊文本从右边开始排列。欧洲的出版物，传统的书脊文本的排列方式是从下至上，而这一规定近来正得到一些改变。书脊通常包含以下4个元素的全部或部分，顺序依次为：（1）作者、编者或编译者；（2）标题；（3）出版商；（4）出版商标志。

在封底内，一直延伸到右页的是后环衬页，它的设计要配合前环衬页，并要和它协调一致，要么是白纸，要么有图案、图像等。封底通常包含作者或编者的传记和它处对本书赞扬的引文，可能还包含该书的内容简介或说明。

Lesson 8 Successful Industrial Design

1. T 2. F 3. F 4. T 5. F

Lesson 9 IDSA

1. B 2. B 3. A 4. B 5. C

Lesson 10 Environmental Design

1. T 2. F 3. T 4. T

Lesson 11 Famous Interior Designers and Their Styles in Interior Design

当你从一个令人惊叹的玻璃大门走进去，你会惊讶于这华丽起居室壮观的室内装饰，穹形天花板和裸露的房梁、大理石壁炉、大浴室、豪华的大理石台面厨房、步入式更衣室和相邻的书房，而瓷砖地板在生活区贯穿流动。落地窗的设计是为了看到柯哈拉海岸和太平洋沿岸山峰的壮丽景色。每一个主卧、客卧和浴室都能透过窗户看到美丽的海景。

Lesson 12 How to Become a Fashion Designer

Ⅰ. 1. F 2. T 3. F 4. T
Ⅱ. 略

Lesson 13 The History of Animation

1. A 2. C 3. A

Lesson 14 The History of Photoshop

虽然Adobe Photoshop是一项几百美元的投资，这一功能强大的图像编辑软件是平面设计师、网页设计师和摄影师的热门选择。该程序的特点是功能的多样化，你可以用它来处理照片或创造新的图像。由于它功能强大，很多专业人士知道Photoshop的高昂费用是一种投资。

色彩校正

Photoshop配有多种工具，像加深、海绵、加亮等工具可以精确地校正色彩。例如，加亮工具可以使图像的局部变亮，而海绵工具可以降低对比度和饱和度。利用这些工具可

以进行局部色彩修正，而不必用于整个图像。该程序还支持彩色与黑白的转换功能，有了它可以调整并保存所喜欢的图像色彩和色调。

选择功能

Photoshop的选择工具允许用户快速便捷地选择一张图像的不同区域。例如，如果想选择一张图像中某人的领带，可以使用磁性套索工具"读取"图像，会紧贴领带的轮廓。像这样对图像特殊部位的选取可以改变图像的个体——在这个案例里，可以轻易地改变领带的颜色而不影响其余部分的图像。

Lesson 15 Dreamweaver and Its Advantages?

 1. F 2. F 3. T

Lesson 16 World Graphic Design Master: Paul Rand

 1. T 2. F 3. F 4. T

Lesson 17 Raymond Loewy — The Man Who Streamlined the Sales-Curve

 1. B 2. C 3. C 4. A

Lesson 18 Frank Lloyd Wright and His Architectures

 略。

Lesson19 Fashion Queen — Coco Chanel

 所有著名的时装和设计的创新都不能超越香奈儿小黑裙的声誉。可可·香奈儿在两次世界大战期间推出了小黑裙，那是一个明亮的色彩和繁琐的花边统治时尚的年代。长袖黑色连衣裙最初用毛料制成用于日间穿着，而绉布、绸缎、天鹅绒制成的小黑裙则用于晚上，就是它震撼了时尚界。后来的小黑裙有了一些变化：短款、无袖、百褶黑色雪纺绸、黑色花边……

 1926年美国《时尚》杂志将可可·香奈儿的小黑裙称为"时尚界的福特"，意味着它的简洁及它巨大的长期成功的潜力。小黑裙被许多女性和时尚观察家认为是一个完整衣橱中必不可少的。香奈儿的小黑裙成为优雅和精致简洁的象征，它的无处不在使得它通常被简称为"LBD"。

Lesson 20　Hayao Miyazaki's Movie World

1. F　2. T　3. F　4. T　5. F

Lesson 21　Landscape Painting in Chinese Art

　　1644年满族入关后，为了掩饰自己明朝皇室后裔的身份，朱耷在一佛寺削发为僧。约在1680年，朱耷还俗回归尘世，开始以绘画和书法为生。1684年，他以"八大山人"作为别号。其一生忠于明朝，八大山人将绘画作为抗议的手段。此画是八大山人在他后二十余年生涯中大胆的、高深莫测作品的典型，他对图像的处理如同书法，注重大与小、实与虚、轻与重的关系，在平面图形和立体空间中创造了一种加强不安感的张力。

Lesson 22　Chinese Folk Art

1. F　2. T　3. T　4. F

Lesson 23　Eric Chan — Finding Balance in Design

　　与赫曼米勒合作所创造的ECCO9709竹制扶手椅，在座位和靠背分别使用了挠曲的竹条，使其舒适，符合人机工程学。支撑部位由三条横向条状聚合物构成——两条横跨靠背，一条横跨座位。其功能就像弹簧，当坐上去时竹条变弯，紧贴身体，当压力减小时反弹到原来的位置。遗憾的是，这一为香港设计中心一个特别展览而制作的椅子仅有15把。然而，陈秉鹏正在继续材料和技术的实验，希望将它变为批量生产的产品。

Lesson 24　Birmingham Institute of Art and Design

住宿

　　学校提供不同地点的学生宿舍遍布伯明翰市，所有的学生宿舍都提供不少于四十周的住宿合同。此外，学校能够提供私人住宅区宿舍详情。对于有特殊需求的学生，在一些学生宿舍设置了专门单位，可根据要求提供进一步的信息。提供的范围包括带厨房的套间，适合研究生和有小家庭学生的单元房。

　　但是不可能保证提供一间学生首选的宿舍，校内宿舍通常优先提供给那些课程是基于该校园的学生。如果房间足够的话，居住在伯明翰地区的全日制学生也会被给予同样的住宿条件。

　　一旦收到住宿通知书，会收到一个住宿包给予更详细的关于膳宿供应的信息，包括一份要完成并返回的申请表格。大多数住宿通知书会在夏季任何优秀的考试结果都证实之后发出。

Lesson 25 Savannah College of Art and Design

　　由于萨凡纳艺术设计学院旨在建立创造性职业的大学，因此学院致力于帮助学生和校友在自己所选择的领域获得成功。事业和校友成功部门可以帮助学生找到实习机会，提供求职援助，并提供广泛的资源来配合求助者找到梦寐以求的工作。

　　如果想获得关于选课的个人指导，或是简历、作品选辑、面试及其他的职位搜索策略等方面的帮助，职业顾问会帮助。本部门还提供关于企业家精神、品牌、薪资谈判、对社会负责的职业生涯等方面的专题研讨会和课程。去年，超过175家的公司和机构来学校会见和招募本校的学生和校友。这些公司进行面试、审核作品辑、发表演讲并参与了教师/学生的网络活动。

参考译文

第1单元 艺术设计史

第1课 工艺美术运动

"不要在你家里放一件你不知其用,或你认为不美的东西。"

——威廉·莫里斯《生活之美》1880

工艺美术运动是一场起源于英国,在1880—1910年年间蓬勃发展的国际设计运动,它的影响力一直持续到20世纪30年代。该运动由艺术家、作家威廉·莫里斯(1834—1896)于19世纪60年代发起,并受到约翰·拉斯金(1819—1900)著作的鼓舞。运动主张忠实于材料,提倡使用简朴形式和具有中世纪的、浪漫的、民俗风格装饰的传统手工艺,以反对机器化大生产所发展出来的设计风格。

该运动受到拉斯金社会批判立场的影响,认为建筑和设计的质量关系到一个国家的道德和社会健康,认为机器是社会罪恶的根源,一个健康的社会取决于技能娴熟和创造性的劳动者。和拉斯金一样,工艺美术运动的艺术家们反对劳动分工,喜欢工艺生产,在手工劳动中整个设计项目是由个人或小集体制作和组装。他们担心伴随着工业的兴起,会带来乡村手工艺的萎缩,并对传统的技能和创造力的丧失感到痛惜。

事实上,工艺美术运动的艺术风格在某种程度上是对1851年世界博览会展示的许多物品的设计风格的一种反抗,这些物品都过分装饰、矫揉造作且忽略了使用材料的品质。艺术史大师尼古拉斯·佩夫斯纳认为博览会中的展品显示出"忽视了图案创作的基本需要和外观的完整性"及"细节上的粗陋"。展览的组织者们亨利·科尔(1808—1882)、欧文·琼斯(1809—1874)、马修·迪格比·怀亚特(1820—1877)和理查德·雷德格雷夫(1804—1888)开始了设计改革,例如,琼斯就曾宣称"装饰……与被装饰物相比必须是次要的","装饰对被装饰物而言必须是恰当的",壁纸和地毯"除了平实和朴素"之外不应有任何其他意味的图案。这些理论被威廉·莫里斯所接受,他认为展览会中的织物和墙纸应该用看起来尽可能真实的自然图案装饰,并且应该是平面化的、简朴的自然图案,就好像威廉·莫里斯的墙纸上所绘制的洋蓟的图案设计那样。为了表现出手工艺的本质之美,有些产品故意留下轻微的未完成的痕迹,以带来某种质朴的效果。

到了19世纪末,工艺美术运动的思想影响到建筑、绘画、雕塑、平面、插图、书籍出版、摄影、室内设计和装饰艺术等领域,涵盖了家具与木制品、彩色玻璃、刺绣和纺织品、珠宝和金属制品。

从1855年开始,这个协会在英国连续不断地举办了一系列的展览,向公众提供了一个了解设计及高雅设计品位的机会,从而促进了"工艺美术"运动的发展。随着在欧洲的广泛展出,工艺美术运动的朴素和忠于材料的品质启发了像亨利·凡德·维尔德这样的设计师及新艺术、维也纳分离派等艺术流派并最终对公立包豪斯学校的创立产生了重大的影响。佩夫斯纳认为该运动是无装饰的简洁形式的现代主义设计的开端。

参考译文

第2课　新艺术运动

　　新艺术运动是一场在艺术、建筑、实用艺术尤其是装饰艺术领域的国际主义风格运动，在20世纪之交的1890—1905年达到流行顶峰。"Art Nouveau"这一名称在法语中为"新艺术"，该运动也被称为"Jugendstil"，即德国的"青年风格"运动，名字来源于促进该运动发展的《青年》杂志。在意大利称为"自由风格"，来源于在伦敦开设的商店——利伯蒂公司，使该风格得到推广。作为对19世纪学院派艺术的一种反抗，它的特点是不仅有高度风格化的流动曲线的形式，而且有以有机的、特别是以花卉等植物为灵感的图案。新艺术运动是艺术家在从建筑到家具等一切工作中，使艺术成为日常生活的一部分的一种设计方法。代表性的作品包括比亚兹莱的插画、麦金托什的家具、高迪的建筑、拉利克的珠宝、路易斯·康福特·蒂凡尼的玻璃器皿及赫克多·吉马德设计的巴黎地铁站入口。

　　这场运动受到捷克艺术家阿方斯·慕夏的深刻影响。当时，阿方斯·慕夏制作了一张用来宣传由剧作家维克托里安·萨尔编剧、杜莎拉·贝恩哈特主演的戏剧《吉丝梦坦》的平版印刷海报，1895年1月1日出现在巴黎的大街上。一夜之间引起轰动，并向巴黎民众宣告新的艺术风格和创始人的诞生。最初被称为慕夏风格，很快成为众所周知的新艺术。

　　伴随着切分音节奏般的弧形曲线形成的动感、起伏感、流动感是新艺术运动最重要的特征，另一个特征就是对双曲线和抛物线的使用。这些传统的装饰线条似乎充满了活力，像是从植物中生长出来的形式。作为一种艺术运动，它与拉斐尔前派和象征主义有着密切联系，可以把像比亚兹莱、阿方斯·慕夏、爱德华·伯恩琼斯、古斯塔夫·克林姆这样的艺术家归类在以上这些风格之中。但是，不同于象征主义绘画，新艺术运动具有鲜明的视觉效果；也不同于过去的工艺美术运动，新艺术运动的艺术家们在纯粹的设计服务中很快接受使用了新材料、使用机器加工外观和抽象的特征。

　　日本木刻版画以其曲线、图案外观、强烈对比的空间和平坦的画面，同样启发了新艺术运动。自此以后，在来自世界各地的艺术家作品中，都能发现某些线条和曲线图案成为绘画中的惯用手段。

　　新艺术运动并没有像工艺美术运动那样否定机器，而是发挥其所长。拿雕塑来说，主要的材料是玻璃和锻铁，甚至使建筑具有了雕塑般的品质。

　　虽然随着20世纪现代主义风格的到来，新艺术运动日渐式微，但是今天它被看作是历史的新古典主义和现代主义之间的重要桥梁。此外，新艺术博物馆现在被联合国教科文组织所认可，在其世界文化遗产清单上作为对文化遗产有重要贡献的项目。拉脱维亚的历史中心里加作为"新艺术运动风格建筑在欧洲最优秀的集合地"，1997年被列入联合国教科文组织名单，其部分原因就是"新艺术/新青年风格建筑的质量和数量"。由维克多·霍塔设计的4个布鲁塞尔的城镇房屋在2000年被列入"人类创造性的天才作品"，是新艺术运动建筑风格的杰出案例，很好地说明了从19世纪到20世纪在艺术、思想和社会方面的变迁。

第3课　构成主义

　　俄国构成主义运动始于1913年，持续到20世纪40年代。它是由俄罗斯前卫艺术家发

起的艺术运动，很快蔓延到欧洲大陆的其他地区。构成主义致力于忠于现代主义的完全抽象，其主题通常是几何图案的、实验性的、理性的。主观或个人主义的形式远比具有普遍意义的客观形式更适合于这场运动。构成的主题也相当微小，艺术作品被分解到其最基本的要素，作品的创作通常使用新媒介，有助于创造一种新的有序的艺术风格。在当时大家都渴望一种新的艺术秩序，因为该运动是在一战刚结束时产生的，提出了对理解、团结与和平的需求。著名的构成主义艺术家包括弗拉基米尔•塔特林、卡西米尔•马列维奇、罗伯特•亚当斯和埃尔•李西茨基。

这个运动的艺术家们受到工业设计的影响并使用这些如金属板和玻璃的工业材料。这些材料通常被用来创建几何形状的物体，这与该运动实用主义的艺术视野保持了一致。

塔特林最著名的作品仍然是他的"第三国际纪念塔"（1919—1920年，莫斯科），一个22英尺高的铁架上附有玻璃材质制作的一个螺旋圆柱、立方体和圆锥体，这原本是大规模的设计。在1917年十月革命之后，塔特林（被认为俄国构成主义之父）为新的苏联教育人民委员部工作，该机构用艺术家和艺术教育公众。在此期间，他研发出了一个官方认可的艺术形式，即"在真实的空间使用真实的材料"。他的第三国际纪念塔项目标志着他首次涉足建筑，并成为了俄国前卫建筑和国际现代主义的象征。

其他的画家、雕塑家、摄影师在这个时期的创作通常使用如玻璃、钢铁、塑料等具有明确定义的工业材料。由于他们对机器、技术、功能主义及现代媒介的赞赏，成员们也被称为艺术家工程师。

第4课　包豪斯及其设计教育

国立包豪斯通常简称为包豪斯，是一所位于德国的将工艺和美术相结合的设计学校，因其宣传和教导的设计方法而出名。包豪斯的经营管理时间从1919年持续到1933年。当时的德语"Bauhaus"字面上是"房屋建筑"的意思，意味着新型的建筑设计体系。

包豪斯学校由沃尔特•格罗佩斯在魏玛成立，尽管它的名字与建筑有关，而且它的创建者事实上就是一位建筑设计师，但是在包豪斯成立的第一年并没有设立建筑系。尽管如此，包豪斯成立的理想是在所有艺术领域包括最终加入进来的建筑领域创造"艺术创作的综合"。包豪斯风格成为现代主义建筑和现代设计最有影响力的潮流之一，它对艺术、建筑、平面设计、室内设计、工业设计和排版艺术后来的发展产生了深远的影响。

学校分设于德国三个城市（1919—1925年的魏玛时期、1925—1932年的德绍时期、1932—1933年的柏林时期），有三任不同的校长：1919—1928年任职的沃尔特•格罗佩斯，1928—1930年任职的汉斯•迈耶，1930—1933年任职的路德维希•密斯•凡德罗。1933年，领导者在纳粹政权的压力下被迫关闭学校。

包豪斯的课程结合了理论教育和在其教学性质的工场进行的实践职业训练。至于老师，也就是包豪斯的大师们，格罗佩斯带来了来自欧洲各地的人，如利奥尼•费宁格、瓦西里•康定斯基、保罗•克利、约翰内斯•伊顿、拉兹洛•莫霍利•纳吉、马歇•布劳耶、汉斯·迈耶和约瑟夫·亚伯斯也加入了教员队伍。

教育过程更多的是为了创新和新的设计典范，并以此作为包豪斯的教育理念。例如，伊顿开发了创新性的"基础课程"，即传授学生关于材料特征、构成和色彩的基础知识。在1920年出版了《色彩艺术》一书，该书所阐述的理念被视为是对阿道夫·霍尔茨尔色彩环的进一步推动。伊顿是第一批成功定义和确定颜色组合策略的人之一，通过他的研究，他发明了利用色相对比的特性使色彩协调的七种方法。

从必修的基础课程开始，学生学习艺术的基础知识（色彩理论、构成、绘画）。在完成了基础课程之后，那时学生开始选择他们所喜欢的专业，在专业化的车间学习建筑学、纺织品设计、家具设计、印刷等。这种教学体系很快被世界各地的艺术设计院校所模仿。学生能够了解制造过程中的问题，了解到人口众多对低成本住房的要求，学习通过织物、家具、用具器皿使室内达到美与功能的统一。

包豪斯学校最大的影响力是在应用设计领域。在这里，设计的是那些工业化批量生产下的日常生活物品，也许设计一个一流的茶壶比一幅二流的绘画要更难。现在的现代设计被尊为一种专业和一种艺术。人们不再为在博物馆里（如纽约现代艺术博物馆）发现现代家具展品而感到惊奇。

第5课　国际主义平面设计风格

国际主义平面设计风格也被称为瑞士风格，是20世纪50年代在瑞士发展起来的平面设计风格，强调整齐、可读性和客观性，是第二次世界大战期间包豪斯原则在苏黎世和巴塞尔的延续发展。该风格发展中的关键人物包括西奥·巴尔莫、马克斯·比尔、马克斯·胡珀，他们所有人都熟悉两次世界大战期间风格派、构成主义和《新版面设计》的前卫设计思想。

该风格理性的特征在于无衬线字体（尤其是赫尔维提加体和通用体）的使用，以及文本被放置在左边精确空白处狭窄的栏内，而放在右边是不合理的。这种简单、几何设想的理性观点通过对摄影图片而不是手绘插图的使用得到进一步的明确。战争期间瑞士的中立地位使得这些设计法则不断发展，并在20世纪50年代、60年代和70年代在国际设计界被越来越多地采纳。

国际主义平面设计风格的影响力通过瑞士出版的《新平面设计》杂志（1958—1965）得到广泛传播，该杂志由约塞夫·穆勒·布鲁克曼、汉斯·纽伯格、理查德·洛斯发行。其版面设计与其出资者所信奉的设计原则一致，是美国许多跨国公司审美的视觉体现。这遭受到新一代的新浪潮平面设计运动的攻击，以更具表现力的、直观的风格作为后现代主义风格的原则，寻求对刻板的瑞士风格的反击。

第2单元　设计专题

第6课　企业形象设计

所有现代的企业家都知道企业形象的重要性。虽然也有一些公司和服务提供商没有

任何企业形象发展战略也获得了成功,但是大多数都会及时意识到要持续到下一阶段的成功,企业形象策划是必需的。如果一家公司决定冒险不关注企业发展,他们将冒着失去现有的消费者忠诚度的危险,并可能面临停滞不前的危险。

大多数情况下,一个企业的形象策划首先从探索和实验阶段开始。在这个阶段,公司可以回顾前期的战略资料,同时也能进行宝贵的消费者研究测试。也有一些公司进行整个管理层访谈以获得他人对公司形象的看法及公司对潜在客户的象征意义。

一旦初始的开发阶段的所有信息得以收集,公司就进入到企业形象发展和定义的过程中。要想获得第二阶段的成功,一些公司组建品牌团队,这些品牌团队除了能够确立任何所需的企业形象之外,同样能够建立企业士气。

在市场营销中,企业形象就是企业的"人格面貌",经过设计以符合和促进商业目标的实现。它通常是通过品牌和商标的使用而明显地表现出来。

当有一个能体现出独特的公司文化即企业人格的共同的组织宗旨时,企业形象便应运而生。在企业形象建立得足够深刻时,公众能够感受到他们拥有该宗旨的所有权。企业形象通常被当作组织的身份,能够帮助公司回答如"我们是谁?"和"我们要去哪里?"这样的问题。企业形象也使消费者能够表达他们对特定的人群聚集或群体的归属感。

总的来说,这就意味着在一套标准内的企业名称、标志、标准字体、色彩及其配套技巧的总和。这些标准控制企业形象如何应用,确定被认可的色彩调色板、字体、版面设计,以及通过该品牌的所有物质表现形式来保持视觉延续性和品牌识别性的其他方法。这些标准通常被规划成一种称为企业识别手册的一套方法。

许多公司如麦当劳和艺电公司在它们所有的产品中都有自己的企业形象,"M"标志及黄色和红色持续出现在整个麦当劳的包装和广告中。许多公司支付了大量的资金用于企业形象的创造研究、设计和执行,以创造出极其独特并吸引目标受众的企业形象。

企业形象通常被视为由三部分组成:

企业形象设计(标志、标准字体、企业色彩等);

企业沟通(广告、公共关系、信息等);

企业行为(内在价值、规范等)。

企业形象建设已经成为促进企业发展和提高企业文化的普遍方法。最著名的是中西元男1968年在日本东京成立的经营战略企业传播委员会和PAOS公司,中西元男在日本发展出融入了设计、经营管理、企业文化的革新的企业形象。在美国,平面设计公司如谢苗耶夫和盖斯马设计公司是将现代设计原则应用到企业形象设计的开拓者。

企业形象似乎是一个具有挑战性的任务,但事实是,通过创造性的思维和对消费者的倾听,甚至最小的公司也能获得企业形象的胜利!

第7课 书籍设计师费奥娜·瑞文

书籍设计师费奥娜·瑞文为世界各地的作家提供了无后顾之忧的书籍设计,包括书籍的封面设计和内页设计。下面的文章来自于她的个人网站。

为了获得创造性的、有益的经验，请参与到你的书籍设计的每一个阶段。我们将会一起将你的想法变为你引以为豪的高品质的书。我将会帮助你避免生产方面代价昂贵的陷阱，并确保你的书在预算之内按时出版。我爱书，也致力使你的书成为最好的。

书籍设计：作者的下一步

你非常努力地完成了你的手稿，并且为下一步做好了准备：将它变为成品书。但是你该从哪里开始呢？——你是一个作家，而不是一个设计师。你之前从未与设计师打交道，这样的任务让你有点不知所措。如果你不满意你的书最终的样子，会发生什么事？并且，如果你并不了解书的生产过程，你将如何知道事情是否步入正轨呢？

享受这个过程

将你的书交给你信任的人，放下关于书籍设计的担心和压力。我知道如何使你的书变得最好。参与到你的书籍设计并看到它的逐步完善，你会喜欢这一创造性的过程。你可以信心十足地将所有的生产细节交给我。

130余本成功的图书项目

我为作者和出版商设计了包括小说、儿童读物、非小说类书籍、摆设书籍在内的130多本图书。我的客户来自于各行各业，大部分都是第一次当作家，有一些是委托设计第二本书、第三本书的老客户，其他的是合作关系固定的出版商。

你会喜欢的一本顶级书

我所有客户的共同点是什么？他们每一个人都得到了一本他们所喜欢的顶级的、专业设计的书籍，同时我在他们的书籍生产的整个过程中给予及时的关注。你也是一样。当你知道你会跟踪你的书籍设计从头到尾的每一个阶段时，你就可以放松了。

我的客户说：

"有可能最好的产品。"

第一次当作家，我很高兴和费奥娜一起工作。她引导我经历每一步进展，并提出我自己从未料想的问题。同时她还在校对、索引、印刷的过程中与我保持联系，她非常注意细节并且想尽可能地开发出最好的作品。她的知识、专业和耐心使设计过程变得轻松和愉快，同时她使我们的愿望得以实现，我们想把我们的书籍再版，再也不会想到与其他人合作。

——杰拉尔丁·布拉奇，药学博士，《克服咳嗽和雷东多海滩的冷空气》的合著者，美国加州

"无人能比的服务水平和产品质量。"

除了费奥娜顶尖的设计能力，她在我们的项目中从始至终所呈现出来的专业素养给了我们极大的信心，这种信心覆盖到公司的每一个基层。我以前与其他设计师也经历过这一过程，可是发现没有人能比得上我们从费奥娜这里所获得的服务水平和产品质量。

——玛丽·麦高，太平洋培训集团副总裁，《了解汤加》的出版者，汤加，努库阿洛法

"信任无价。"

与费奥娜一起为我的书籍进行第二版的工作，比另一机构为我的第一版工作所获得的经历要好得多。费奥娜很平易近人，没有重大的耽搁，她一直陪着我。此外，当我要求修改时我从来没有感觉到我正在烦扰她。事实上，她一直是如此的平静和让人放心，和她交谈后我往往感觉比之前更放松。对于一位要将他的作品交给他人的紧张作家来说，这种程度的信任是无价的！

——妲雅·阿尔泰·皮尔思，《智战癌症：替代性无毒性的治疗方法》的作者，美国内华达州斯泰特莱恩

保证满意

如果我们一起为你的书工作，我相信你会对书的质量和我所提供的服务水平非常满意。事实上，我保证会如此。

为你的书征求报价

访问我的询价页，然后打电话或发电子邮件来讨论你的书——完全免费。如果你愿意，我可以在我们的讨论结束后给你一个正式的报价。

记住，你的书籍的出版之路并不一定充满坎坷！它可以是一路创造性的、有益的和无故障的。

第8课　成功的工业设计

工业设计是实用艺术和应用科学的结合体，据此，美学、人机工程学和产品的可用性可以提高销售和生产。工业设计师用艺术学、营销学、工学设计日常生活品——从智能手机到医疗设备再到家庭用品等。每一天，人们都要依赖工业设计师们设计的产品。正是这些设计师们负责产品的风格、功能（或可用性）、质量及安全。

术语"工业设计"经常被认为出自设计师约瑟夫·克劳德·西奈尔（尽管他本人在后来的采访中否认），但是这门学科居先于此至少10年之久。它的起源在于消费品的产业化。例如，包豪斯的先驱——1907年成立的并得到国家支持的德意志制造联盟，致力于将传统工艺和工业化大生产技术相结合，将德国推上了与英国和美国激烈竞争的地位。

工业设计同样关注技术概念、产品和工艺。除了考虑美观、可用性和人机工程外，它还包含产品工程设计、实用性、市场投放，还有诸如诱惑、心理、欲望及用户对产品的情感依恋等其他问题。

产品开发看上去是一个艰巨的任务，但是如果了解了所需的基本步骤和阶段，一切就会变得简单得多。成功的工业设计可分为7个步骤。

问题评估

写下什么是首要问题，这是一个好主意，但是这个时候，即使知道如何去做也不要写下问题的解决方法。只需要说明是什么问题，仅此而已。本人曾看到仅仅因为这个问题从

未被写下来而使新产品的开发变得复杂而耗时。问题的适当陈述有助于保持每个人意见一致,并能够避免项目进展缓慢。

设计详述

这是对先前已明确问题开始形成解决方案的一步。这时候,一切所能想到的需求清单应该被写下来,并不是提出一个只是为了解决产品生产的需求的解决方案。清单上应该罗列的内容包括:零售价格(人们愿意为它支付多少钱),物体的大小(是否需要去适应某人的手或是能够通过一扇门或进入车库),它的速度应该有多快,它是否需要防水,它应该由什么材料制作,它是使用电池还是墙上的插头。这份清单可以无穷无尽,重要的是列出什么对企业来说很重要。这份清单将会在下一步对企业和设计师有所帮助。

创意的产生

此阶段问题已经明确,需求也已设置。这时应该集思广益进行头脑风暴并概述想法,不要担心图纸不够漂亮,只是要看概念能否实现或是否有明显的缺陷。如果对机械不在行,可能要找专攻产品或工业设计的人帮忙。在有义务签署一份合同或支付费用之前,许多设计公司能够积极参与,讨论并勾勒一些想法。在进入到下一个步骤之前,还可以想出一两个好主意。

概念设计

一旦至少一个关于新产品的好想法得以拟定,就会想了解设计工作中更多的细节。设计师会在计算机上提供一个足够详细以确保创意实现的基本的三维设计,但不会过于详细,因为它不是仅仅几个小时就能完成的。这一步是想法要么通过,要么被丢弃的最后阶段。

细节设计

既然一个好的概念设计已被创造出来,是开始认真考虑细节的时候了。在这个阶段,设计师将建立各部分完整详细的三维虚拟模型,解决设计上的问题,绘制装配线和各零件图纸,找到所有要购买的零部件的供应商,如果有必要,创造三维样品。当所有问题都得到解决,全套图纸已经交付时,这个阶段就完成了。

测试

测试是产品设计中极为重要的一部分,不可忽视。这一步骤可以简单到让一部分人使用产品以得到反馈信息,也可以复杂到将它送到像保险商试验所这样的测试研究所,由专业人员进行全面检测。该级别的测试极大地取决于将要出售该产品的零售商的要求。重要的是要找到没有参与设计过程的其他人来测试产品,即使他是朋友也不行。没有参与设计的他人可以提出中肯的意见,这样就可以注意他们在使用产品过程中可能会遇到的所有困难。

制造

设计过程中的最后一个步骤就是制造,在这一步,企业或设计师将寻找适合的生产设备以创造该产品。需要根据制造商所提供的产品、需要支付的费用及产品何时交货达成协议。

第9课 美国工业设计师协会

美国工业设计师协会（IDSA）是世界上历史最悠久、最大的、会员主导性最强的产品设计、工业设计、交互设计、工效学、设计研究、设计管理、通用设计及相关设计领域的协会。该协会每年组织著名的工业设计优秀奖（IDEA）竞赛，每年主办一次国际设计会议和五个地区会议，出版了设计类的季刊杂志《创新》及电子周报*Design bytes*，关注设计界最新的新闻资讯。美国工业设计协会的慈善机构即设计基金会，每年资助各地在校大学生奖学金以继续接受工业设计教育。

卡罗尔·冈茨（美国工业设计师协会特别会员）于1979—1980年担任协会主席。在他为协会所做的诸多贡献之中，包括他为美国工业设计师协会网站提供了设计历史的内容——《设计100年》。

该专业化的设计师组织可以追溯到专业本身的开端阶段，在1927年第一次得到美国公众的注意。那一年，纽约的梅西家族举办了一场引起广泛注意的商业艺术展，该展览以"现代产品"为特征。其中许多物品来自1925年在巴黎举办的国际装饰艺术和现代工业艺术展，作为重要的"现代主义运动"迟迟得到美国政府的认可。

很快地，公众和制造商对这种新的装饰艺术风格的要求如此迫切、需求如此之大，使得许多设计人员（通常是建筑师、包装设计师或舞台设计师）将他们的创造力第一次放在了大批量生产的产品上。他们宣称了一个新的头衔"工业设计师"，源于1913年，美国专利局作为当时通用的"工业中的艺术"这一词的同义词而出现的。

一些设计师很快成立了美国装饰艺术家和工匠同盟（AUDAC），以保护他们工业化、装饰性的实用艺术，并展出他们的新作品。美国装饰艺术家和工匠同盟吸引了大量的艺术家、设计师、建筑师、商业机构、工业公司和制造商。在几年内，拥有了100余个会员，并在1930—1931年间举办了很多大型的展览。

1933年，国家家具设计师委员会（NFDC）成立，与家具代理商和设计师一起为国家复兴管理部门（NRA）起草了一个法规，以防止设计的剽窃行为。但是在1934年，国家复兴管理部门被宣布违反章程，国家家具设计师委员会也随即解散。

1936年，芝加哥的美国家具拍卖场邀请首席设计师成立一个新的被称为"美国家具设计师协会"的组织。很多成员感觉受到了只针对家具工业单一的赞助的限制，1938年他们成立了一个基础更为宽泛的组织，称为美国设计师协会（ADI），允许专攻诸多设计领域中的一种门类，包括手工艺、装饰艺术、平面设计、产品设计、包装设计、展览及自发的风格等。约翰·沃尔索斯（1898—1985）担任美国设计师协会的首任主席。

1944年2月，东海岸15位杰出的设计从业者成立了工业设计师协会（SID），每一个创立者在第二年邀请另外一位设计师加入。对会员的要求是严苛的，要求设计至少三种不同工业领域的批量化生产的产品。工业设计师协会成立的部分原因是为了加强工业设计专业的合法化，并严格要求会员们是有经验的专业人士。沃尔特·道文·提革担任工业设计师协会的首任主席。

1951年，美国设计师协会将它的管理中心迁到了纽约，在此过程中吸收了芝加哥工业设计师协会（CSID），并将其更名为工业设计师协会（IDI），那一年，协会开始颁发一年一度的国家设计奖，一直持续到1965年。到1962年前，工业设计师协会在美国的10个分会已经拥有350个会员。

1955年，工业设计师协会（SID）更名为全美工业设计师协会（ASID）。到1962年，协会在国家的4个分会拥有约100个会员。

1957年，因为两个专业性的组织（工业设计师协会和全美工业设计师协会）将教育家吸收为会员，工业设计教育联合会（IDEA）成立。它的首任主席是约瑟夫·卡雷罗（1920—1978）。

经过十多年的仔细协商，1965年工业设计师协会（IDI）、全美工业设计师协会（ASID）和工业设计教育联合会（IDEA）合并组成了美国工业设计师协会（IDSA）。为了这样做，各自的实力、目的、理念合并成了美国工业设计统一的声音。

今天，美国工业设计师协会在美国、英国和中国拥有3 300个会员，28个分部，17个特别兴趣小组及30多个学生分会。会员们经常相互联系，并作为行业的领导者与世界各地其他的公司、设计机构、政府互相影响。

第10课　环境设计

我们都知道哪些地方是我们宁可不居住的或是感觉不自在的，也许是因为我们不喜欢这个建筑，也许是因为它的肮脏和混乱，又或许是有室内空气污染。事实上，不幸的是它已经变成了生活中的事实。现在，环境设计能够解决以上问题。

环境设计是实用艺术和创造人类设计环境的科学。这些领域包括建筑、城市规划、园林景观和室内设计，也包括诸如历史建筑保护和灯光设计等跨学科领域。从更大的范围而言，环境设计还涉及工业产品设计：创新型的汽车、风力发电机、太阳能电力设备及其他类型的设备都能够作为这方面的范例。目前，这个词已经扩展到可适用于生态和可持续发展问题。

环境设计概念的溯源首先就是公元前500年左右在古希腊开始的太阳能加热。当时，大多数希腊人耗尽了木材燃料，使得建筑师设计能够捕获太阳光能的房子。希腊人了解到太阳的位置一年四季各不相同。北纬40度的夏天，太阳在南边70度的天顶角处，很高。然而在冬天，太阳以26度的天顶角在一个较低的轨迹运行。希腊的房屋前面朝南，在夏天很少或几乎没有太阳，但在冬季得到充足的阳光，使房屋温暖。此外，朝南的方位保护房屋免受寒冷北风的吹袭。这种聪明的房屋布局影响了古代城市网格布局的使用。由于房屋是南北朝向，希腊城市的街道主要是东西朝向。

罗马人继续太阳能建筑实践，同样是因为在公元前一世纪罗马人在他们本土的意大利半岛上过度砍伐。罗马单词"heliocaminus"，字面意思为"太阳能炉"，与早期希腊房子有同样的功能。众多的公共浴室面向南方，罗马建筑师在窗户上加上玻璃，让光线通过，并且由于热量无法逃离，以保持室内温度。罗马人还利用温室全年种植农作物，种植了来自于帝国僻远角落的各种奇异植物。老普林尼写到大棚温室提供了皇帝台比留斯厨房一年的供应。

随着太阳能建筑和玻璃作为太阳能集热器的使用，古人知道了利用太阳能的其他方式。希腊人、罗马人和中国人发明了曲面的反射镜，可以集中足够强的太阳光线于物体上，使其在几秒钟内燃烧。这种太阳能反射镜往往由银、铜或黄铜制成。

现代环境设计的早期根源始于19世纪末的作家、设计家威廉·莫里斯，他在自己工作室的墙纸、织物和书籍的生产中拒绝使用工业化的材料和程序。他和其他的人，如约翰·拉斯金感觉到工业革命将会给大自然和工人带来伤害。

菲尔·柯西诺的叙事纪录电影《生态设计：创造未来》声称在第二次世界大战后的几十年中，"世界被迫面对科学和工业的阴影"。从20世纪中期，如巴克明斯·特富勒的思想家扮演了催化剂的作用，拓展和深化了环境设计师们的关注点。如今，能源效率、适当的技术、有机园艺与农业、土壤改良、新城市主义、生态的可持续性能源和废物系统得以被考虑，各自获得应用。

通过将可再生能源如太阳能光电、光热甚至是地热能源结合到建筑结构中，创建零排放建筑是可能的，该建筑自我生成所消耗的能源是无污染的。还可以建造"加能建筑"，所产生的能量多于它们所消耗的能量，过剩的可以出售给电网。在美国，LEED绿色建筑评估体系对建筑的评价就是基于对环境的可持续发展基础之上的。

环境设计过程的案例包括利用道路噪声计算模型设计隔音屏障，利用道路空气扩散模型分析与设计城市交通公路。有意识在此理念和实践框架内工作的设计师将生态作为其设计依据，寻求自然与技术的融合。一些人认为保护、管理和再生策略可以应用于从个人建筑到社区建筑的所有级别的规模，有利于人类个体、当地及全球的生态系统。

第11课　著名的室内设计师及他们的室内设计风格

20世纪是著名的室内设计师们开始得到公众认可的时期。事实上，室内设计行业在20世纪后期才开始得以发展。直到那个时候，室内设计还是一个几乎无人知晓的行业。不能否认的是室内设计界并不像时尚界那样的多产，然而，仍然有许多有进取心和创造精神的人们是以有影响力的专业的室内设计而著名的，有好几个甚至为富裕的精英阶层客户而设计。

在世界不同地区的许多著名的室内设计师因他们独特的风格而闻名。其中一个设计师叫妮娜·坎贝尔，当她12岁时，她和她的母亲总是在晚餐后重新摆放家具。这种无法控制的习惯很可能造就了妮娜在美化、复兴与装饰方面的天赋。当妮娜为约翰·福勒（一个与著名的壁纸和织物设计公司相关联的名称）工作时，即Colefax and Fowler公司，她在室内装饰领域内的职业生涯开始了。妮娜的父亲是维也纳人，母亲是苏格兰人，在一个非常国际化的环境中长大，因此，她的风格着重舒适和奢华。"我喜欢融合现代和传统的作品，或许是将传统家具和新布料搭配。我会永远记得约翰·福勒在Colefax and Fowler公司时说的：'装饰时不要夺去房间的生命，给它呼吸的空间，并使它具有自己的个性！'"妮娜说。妮娜的风格加上她的面料感和色彩感帮助她在职业生涯中取得了很大的进步。现在她是全球领先的室内设计师之一,设计业务包括织品、装饰品、壁纸,还包括其他的如家具、餐桌用布和礼品包装等项目。

意大利的莫罗·里帕里尼是另一位杰出的室内设计师,他最为著名的是他的"自然极简"风格。莫罗·里帕里尼风格的特点是快乐、喜悦的美好面,他对色彩的大胆使用和创新的视觉概念表达出了艺术原理。他还为工业设计产业的发展作出了若干值得称道的贡献,包括对日本和欧洲声望较高的公司开发的产品。他已经在他的职业生涯中赢得了荣誉,包括科隆国际杜邦奖和米兰青年设计师奖。

还有另一个知名的室内设计师是瑞秋·安斯韦尔,她作为"旧物别致"风格的拥有者和创始人,同时也是同名电视节目的主持人被普遍认同。"旧物别致"是反映安斯韦尔装饰倾向的一个术语,用任何物品从陈旧的家具到新的桌子、沙发、地毯和灯具来装饰家居,她给予了舒适感也给予了精致感。安斯韦尔通常喜欢将奶油色和白色、淡粉色、绿色和蓝色结合使用。受益于安斯韦尔独特的设计才能的名人中有几个顶级的名字,包括歌手詹妮弗·洛佩兹、麦当娜、安东尼·霍普金斯和朱莉娅·罗伯茨等明星都是她的追捧者。

一个为室内设计界增添光彩,并且满足丰富和著名需求的值得庆祝的名字来自中东,他就是在以色列出生的路昂·阿拉德。路昂·阿拉德在20世纪80年代作为自学成才的制造商和雕塑般家具的设计师获得声望。他是位于意大利科莫的阿拉德工作室的创造者,他的作品出现在世界各地许多建筑与设计的出版物中,其作品还在许多画廊和展览馆展出。

第12课 如何成为一名时装设计师

时装设计往往是吸引年轻人的职业,那些在年轻时期花了大量时间阅读时尚杂志或是给她们的洋娃娃做衣服的人们,通常在她们成为成年人之前就知道把时装设计作为职业是一种兴趣的吸引力使然。然而,要想锤炼成这个领域成功的职业人,仍然有许多专业方面和其他事情要去了解。本文就工作职责、薪资水平、工作前景提供专业概述,同时还阐述了成为一名顶级时装设计师所需要的技能、培训和其他要求。

一名时装设计师要做些什么?

时装设计师是消费者每年花费数十亿美元购买的服装和相关配饰的创造者。在这一个过程中,设计者通常要学习了解时尚流行趋势、草图设计、色彩及面料选择,还要全局监管从最初的设计到新服装、配饰的最终完成这一个过程。一些时装设计师专注于服装设计(男装、女装、童装),鞋子设计(鞋子和靴子),或者是配饰设计(手提包、皮带、围巾、帽子、袜子等),而其他人则在所有时装设计的门类中进行创造性设计。

时装设计师根据他们的经验水平及他们工作的公司的规模大小,在这些步骤的部分或全部的过程中会呈现不同水平的参与。一些时装设计师(大约25%)自己就是经营者,他们通常根据合同为个人代理工作。这种类型的设计师往往工作时间偶然性强,通常需要调整自己的工作时间来适应客户的计划安排和最后期限。其他的设计师被工厂、批发商或设计公司雇用,为大众市场进行设计。这种类型的设计师即使他们偶尔需要工作超长时间来满足生产期限或是为服装秀做准备,但往往他们工作计划常规。最顶级的时装设计师受雇于纽约和加利福尼亚。该行业的全球性要求不断地满足整个美国和全世界的供应商、制

造商和消费者，以及定期出席贸易和时装表演。结果就是大部分的时尚设计师能够经常旅行。时装设计的收入根据雇主和工作经验有很大的区别。刚入行的时装设计师通常开始是作为有经验的设计师的样板师或草图助手，往往收入较低，直到在这个行业的地位得以建立并得到更高的职位。领固定薪水的设计师要比自我创业的设计师收入更高更稳定。然而，一小部分能够获得成功的创业的时装设计师要比拿固定薪水的工资最高的设计师的收入还要高很多倍。

成为时装设计师所要遵循的步骤是什么？

学会绘图和缝纫。在家里开始绘制服装创意草图，保存这些草图并经常修改，还要学习色彩及如何有效地搭配它们。除了绘图能力外，时装设计师还需要有缝纫和样板制作技能，即使设计师并不一定就是直接完成这些工作的人。设计师要能够了解这些技能，这样他们才能正确监督服装的制造。同样，如果客户能够从草图开始一直看到设计的完成，设计也会给人更深刻的印象。

尽可能了解与行业有关的每一件事。了解服装公司及每个公司制作服装的设计风格，了解时尚趋势并努力预测未来的流行趋势，到知名的大百货公司及卖特殊时尚用品的店了解服装的销售，同时还要熟悉消费者（年龄、收入、生活品味等）及消费者的购买需求。

接受学校教育。很多学院、大学、私立艺术与设计学校提供时装设计的学士学位及相关学位的课程。要计划在任何一个时装设计的教学上花费至少两年的时间。经认可的大学水平的所有课程清单可以从国家艺术与设计学校协会获得。一个很聪明的做法是在获得了一个时装设计学位后再加修一个商务和市场营销学位或时装营销采购学位。强大的销售力、演讲技巧和时尚界最后的业务知识对于成功的职业生涯是非常重要的。

建立一个原创设计的作品集。一个人的最佳设计作品的作品选辑是他/她的创造力的最好展示，也能更接近令人信服的潜在雇主，相信此人将是他们的商业资产。作品集可以在很早就开始，最好是毕业之前，应该尽可能包含最广泛的各种不同的工作。

尽可能获得行业经验。这可以在早期的志愿者工作中就获得。为社区剧院做戏剧服装是如何在行业起步的一个例子。在设计公司或是制造公司的实习将证明是非常宝贵的行业经验。为了获得更多的经验，第一份工作是样板师或是有经验的设计师的草图助手的收入并不可观，但将是非常值得的，将为职业生涯阶梯上的不断攀升做好准备。

如何成为一名优秀的时尚设计师？

学习与设计有关的软件程序的知识。在当今世界，CAD软件及像Adobe Photoshop和Illustrator这样的程序软件为时尚设计师提供了重要的能力。重要的是要尽可能地广泛熟悉各种不同的软件程序。

订阅商业报纸和时尚杂志。这是紧跟时尚潮流的好方法。业内专业人士定期专研这些出版物，成功的时尚设计师也应该如此。

制造尽可能多的行业联系。这些联系中有许多可以在学校就得以发展，要包括相关领域的人们，如广告界。

　　成为一名优秀的时装设计师的资质包括对色彩和细节敏锐的眼睛、平衡感和比例感及对美的鉴赏能力。时装设计师不仅需要画图技能，同样更需要良好的沟通和解决问题的能力，但是最重要的是要知道什么是工作需要，以及为了职业成功所需要采取的步骤。职业生涯准备过程中知识全面的人将会成为行业的领跑者，并能够期待开始一个有趣和有回报的职业生涯。

第13课　动画的历史

　　动画如今是已经闯入电影产业的一个词汇。每一个人，从8岁的小孩到80岁的老爷爷都喜欢看动画电影。是否曾想过究竟什么是动画及它又是如何产生的呢？动画基本上是一连串形象、二维或三维作品、模拟场景的快速显示。这种显示如此之快从而能够创造观众的运动幻觉。这种视觉暂留现象就是动画发展的主要依据。如果想进一步探讨动画的起源和历史，请看下面提供的信息。

　　动画的最早的实例可以追溯到旧石器时代，当时试图以绘画的方式捕捉动作。当时的洞穴绘画描绘叠加的动物，以达到绘制传达运动知觉的目的。视觉暂留，动画背后的基础，是由希腊天文学家托勒密在公元130年发现的。50年后的公元180年，一个身份不明的中国发明家发明了早期的动画装置，这就是人们后来才知道的西洋镜。

　　费纳齐镜、实用镜和手翻书是在19世纪时期发明的其他早期的动画装置，所有这些装置技术手段的使用都是用于产生连续的图画运动的目的。但是，直到19世纪90年代晚期电影胶片的引入才推动了动画概念的发展。没有一个人可以享用动画的"创造者"这一头衔。这是因为在动画的发展历程中，很多人同时参与了同样的事情。

　　詹姆斯·斯图尔特·布莱克顿是制作动画电影的第一人，他称这部电影为《滑稽的面部表情》。为了达到这一目的，他曾经在黑板上绘制了一个接一个的滑稽面孔，并将它们拍摄下来。1910年，爱米尔·科尔创作出了第一部剪纸动画。在1913年左右，电影胶片的发展使动画更容易掌控。在谈到动画的历史时，三个绝对值得一提的名字是美国的温瑟·马凯、法国的爱米尔·科尔和乔治·梅里爱。

　　爱米尔·科尔的《幻影集》（1908年）是第一部使用传统（手绘）动画制作的动画电影。特技电影的创作者乔治·梅里爱是将动画和特技运用在一起的第一人，并提出了逐格动画的想法。温瑟·马凯也创造了许多动画电影，最著名的是《小尼莫》（1911年）、《恐龙格蒂》（1914年）和《路斯坦尼雅号之沉没》（1918年）。事实上，很多人将《路斯坦尼雅号之沉没》视为第一部动画故事片。

　　但是，是华特·迪士尼将动画推向了一个全新的水平。1928年，随着《威利汽船》的首映，他成为第一个将声音添加到电影卡通片的动画师。华特·迪士尼在1937年取得的另一个里程碑，是他制造出的第一个完整长度的动画电影，名为《白雪公主和七个小矮人》。1955年阿特·克罗雷创造了《古比》，一个逐格的黏土动画。计算机的介入标志着动画概念的进一步发展。

　　1951年，伊凡萨瑟兰麻省理工学院的学生创造了一个计算机绘图程序——绘图板，进一步推动了动画的发展。随着时间的推移，计算机在动画领域的地位开始日益重要，就像

电影《星球大战》中的许多特殊效果依赖于计算机动画。1995年，由华特迪士尼制片公司和皮克斯动画工作室制作的第一部完整的动画故事长片《玩具总动员》，完全是在计算机上绘制的。自从那时起，动画及计算机携手共进创建时代的新的里程碑。

第14课　Photoshop的历史

1988年9月，诺尔兄弟的运气改变了。约翰向Adobe公司的内部创意团队提交了一个演示版，他们喜欢这个产品。不久后达成了许可证协议，经过10个月的开发，Photoshop 1.0于1990年2月发货了。

托马斯一直参与这一项目，他从来就没有时间完成他的论文。约翰继续他在工业光学魔术公司的职业生涯，任视觉效果总监完成了如《碟中谍》《星际旅行：第一类接触》《星球大战前传：魅影危机》等影片。格伦·诺尔仍然作为教授在密歇根大学工程学院任教。但他现在在家里使用的是Powerbook G3，而地下室的暗房已经被替换为——是的，你猜对了——Photoshop这一图像处理软件。

开始

1987年，约翰·诺尔正在工业光学魔术——卢卡斯电影公司为《星球大战》新成立的特效部门工作。而托马斯正在密歇根大学就图像处理的博士学位进行研究工作，他刚刚购买了一台全新的苹果计算机来帮助写论文，他沮丧地发现在单色显示器上无法显示灰度图像，所以，就像真正的黑客那样，他着手编写自己的代码来完成这项工作。

一点也不令人惊讶，约翰还在ILM致力于图像处理的工作。在一次假期的探望中，他对托马斯的进展印象深刻。在《CG101：计算机图表产业参考》一书中约翰说道："当汤姆向我展示他的工作时，我突然想起它与皮克斯的图像处理工具多么相似。"因此，两人在更大更具结合力的应用程序上开始合作，该程序被他们振奋人心地称为Display。

没过多久，约翰买了一台全新的彩色Macintosh II并说服托马斯修改Display，使其能以彩色模式工作。事实上，约翰看到的Display的次数越多，他就开始要求更多的功能：伽玛校正、加载和保存其他文件格式等。

虽然这项工作分散了托马斯的论文工作，但是他很乐意效劳。他还开发了一种能够进行选择并只影响图像局部的创新方法，同时还有一组图像处理例程——这在后来成为插件。伴随着对色彩平衡、色相、色彩饱和度控制的色调调整功能也出现了，这些是Photoshop的本质特征，但在当时，在实验室或是在ILM以外的任何地方看到专业处理软件几乎是不可想象的。

到了1988年，Display的名字变成了ImagePro，并且足够成熟以至于约翰认为他们会有机会将它作为一种商业应用程序出售。托马斯不是很情愿，他还没有完成他的论文，创造一个完善的应用程序将需要大量的工作。但是在约翰调查了为数不多的竞争者后，他们意识到ImagePro超越了目前现有的任何一款图像处理软件。

从ImagePro到Photoshop

于是，他们开始寻找投资者。托马斯不断改变软件名称，但毫无意义，只是找到一个已经在其他地方已被使用的名字。没有人能够完全确定Photoshop这个名字最初从何而来，但据说，它是由一个潜在的出版商提出的，然后沿用下来。非常偶然，正好当时早期版本的启动画面上显示为Photoshop的名称——这似乎更为符合目前外来资本的热潮。

回想起来值得注意的是，大多数软件公司对Photoshop嗤之以鼻，或者是已经在开发自己的类似应用程序。只有Adobe公司愿意采用它，但是一个合适的交易不是那么容易的。然而最终，一个名为Barneyscan的扫描仪制造商决定将它与扫描仪捆绑在一起，以Barneyscan XP的名字卖出了少量。

对数码图像的未来来说，幸运的是这不是一个长期的合同。约翰很快回到Adobe公司以争取更多利益，在那里他会见了拉塞尔·布朗，当时的艺术总监，对程序印象深刻并说服公司采用。不管是Photoshop公司天真或是诺尔兄弟精明，Photoshop没有被买断所有权，Adobe公司只有发行权，版税仍属于诺尔兄弟。

这项协议好像并没有意味着诺尔兄弟能够坐下来放松一下，如果有什么区别的话，他们现在必须要更努力地为一个官方的1.0版本的发行做准备。托马斯继续开发所有主要应用程序的代码，而约翰独自参与一些插件的开发，使一些认为这些不过是噱头的Adobe公司的工作人员感到惊愕。

奇怪的是这种态度仍然存在于一些纯粹主义者中，他们声称大多数Photoshop的插件某种程度上是"欺骗"，在任何情况下都不会去触碰。而在使用得当时，其他的人还是对插件的灵活性和功能深信不疑。

在程序形成的这些日子里，由于总是要添加一些新的功能，托马斯不得不腾出时间来编写代码。在约翰的鼓励下，拉塞尔·布朗很快成为Photoshop最大的传道士，以及在Adobe公司其他创意人员的努力下，应用程序慢慢形成了，它最终于1990年2月投放市场。

第15课 Dreamweaver及其优点

Adobe Dreamweaver（以前称为Macromedia Dreamweaver）是最初由Macromedia公司创建的网站开发应用程序，现在由Adobe公司开发，该公司在2005年收购了Macromedia公司。

Dreamweaver是可以让使用者输入文本并将媒体元素直接添加到页面的网页设计程序，就像使用微软Word的文字处理程序一样。它能够将文本和图形页面设计转换成由网络浏览器读取的HTML代码，它能够适用于Mac和Windows操作系统。最新版本已经加入了像CSS和JavaScript这样的网页技术支持和包括ASP、ColdFusion和PHP在内的各种服务器端脚本语言和框架。

Dreamweaver允许用户在本地安装的网络浏览器上预览网站。它提供了传输和同步功能，在整个网站中通过搜索词和正确表达能够查找和替换文本或代码行，允许没有服务器端或脚本的单一源代码的共享、整个网站的布局更新的模板特征。行为面板能够使没有任何编程知识的用户使用基本的JavaScripts成为可能。还可以与Adobe的Spry Ajax框架集成，可轻松获得动态生成的内容和界面。

艺术设计专业英语

  Dreamweaver可以使用第三方"扩展"来扩展应用程序的核心功能，任何网站开发人员都可以编写（主要在HTML和JavaScript环境）。Dreamweaver被许多扩展开发者所支持，他们可以为大多数网站开发任务（商业和免费兼有）提供扩展功能，从简单的滑动效果到功能齐全的网上购物。

  Dreamweaver是一个高度互动的网页编辑器，让用户可以无须了解HTML或任何代码就能够创建高度动态的网站。然而，如果这是他们所擅长的，有经验的用户可以使用代码。如果学习Dreamweaver的技巧，如"拖拽及放下"，网站的建设工作会变得非常容易。一个图形用户界面允许用户利用非常复杂的脚本技术构建高度先进的网站。

  下面是对Dreamweaver提供的一些功能的简单总结：

  网站管理——集成文件传输给客户端、允许站点导航的可视化站点地图、文件链接、网站的上传和同步。

  模板——模板使用户能快速编辑整个网站的所有常见元素，如导航栏。

  层叠样式表——让用户快速改变整个网站的文本元素外观。

  JavaScript行为——Dreamweaver的行为代码是用户可以申请的JavaScripts代码，而无须处理这些必需的代码。

第3单元　设 计 大 师

第16课　世界平面设计大师保罗·兰德

  保罗·兰德是美国著名的平面设计师，因他的企业标志设计而闻名。兰德曾在普拉特学院（1929—1932年）、帕森斯设计学院（1932—1933年）和艺术学生联盟（1933—1934年）学习。他是瑞士平面设计风格的发起人之一。从1956—1969年，又于1974年开始，兰德在康涅狄格州纽黑文市的耶鲁大学担任设计教师。兰德于1972年入选了纽约艺术指导俱乐部名人堂。他设计了许多海报和企业形象，包括为IBM公司、UPS快递公司和美国广播公司设计的标志。兰德1996年因癌症逝世。

  当兰德于82岁去世时，他的职业生涯长达60年，经历了设计史的众多篇章。早在1932年还只有十几岁时，他就开始努力提高平面设计行业使其从手工艺艺术成为专业技能。在20世纪40年代早期，他就对广告、书籍、杂志及包装设计的实践产生影响。到了40年代末，他研制出了一种形式单纯的设计语言，一种曾经唯一盛行的风格和技巧。

早期的生活和教育

  保罗·兰德于1914年出生于纽约布鲁克林。由于正统的犹太教法律禁止可作为偶像崇拜的雕刻图像的创作，兰德创造全球资本主义崇拜的图像符号的职业生涯看起来几乎是不可能的。在他还非常年轻的时候，他就欣然接受为父亲的杂货店和学校绘制图形。兰德的父亲不相信艺术能够维持儿子足够的生计，因此，他要求保罗在参加了普拉特学院夜校课程的同时还进入曼哈顿的Harren高中学习，然而这两所学校都没有给兰德太多的启发。尽管在普拉特和纽约地区的其他学校进行学习（包括帕森斯设计学院和纽约艺术学生联盟），兰德总的来说是"自学成才的设计师，从欧洲的杂志如《实用绘图》上学习卡桑德拉和莫霍利·纳吉的作品"。

早期事业

他的事业从卑微的任务开始，兼职为一个财团创造股票图表，将图表提供给各种各样的报纸和杂志。在他20岁出头时，他的作品开始赢得国际赞誉。著名的是他为《方向》杂志设计的封面，兰德的设计不收取费用，以换取充分的艺术自由。

虽然兰德是因他在20世纪50年代和60年代所设计的企业标志而著名，但是他早期的版面设计是他声誉的最初来源。1936年，兰德得到为《服装艺术》杂志的周年特刊设计版面的工作。"他非凡的天赋使得平凡的照片变成充满活力的创作，赋予了版面排版的重要性"，并使兰德获得了一项全职的工作，在23岁那年接任《君子》杂志的艺术总监。

企业形象

无可否认，兰德对平面设计最广为人知的贡献是他的企业形象设计，其中很多至今仍在使用。IBM公司、美国广播公司、康明斯发动机公司、西屋电器公司、UPS快递公司和其他许多公司一样，都是兰德的图形财产，虽然UPS快递公司最近对兰德的经典设计进行了一次有争议的更新。正如莫霍利·纳吉所指出的那样，他的主要优势之一就是他能够像销售员那样阐述他为公司所做的形象需求。

兰德关于企业形象的概念来自于1956年他所设计的IBM标志，就像马克·斐弗曼所说："不仅仅是一个身份，而是渗透了企业意念和公众意识的基本的设计理念"。兰德1962年修改了该标志，1972年把它变为有条纹的标志。从20世纪70年代初直到80年代初，兰德还为IBM公司设计包装和营销资料，包括著名的"Eye-Bee-M"海报。

理论的发展

保罗迅速出名不仅仅是因为他的设计，同样是因为他的设计理念。尽管在他职业生涯的不同阶段有一大群工作人员，兰德在他的创作过程中是独处的，承载着大多数的设计工作。他对于出版理论书籍阐述他的设计理念非常感兴趣。

显而易见的是，杜威是兰德平面设计基本观点的重要理论来源。在兰德的第一本著作《关于设计的思考》的第一页，作者一开始关于现代艺术功能性审美的完美需求就来自于杜威的哲学。兰德在《关于设计的思考》中提出的设计思想之一是即使模糊不清或残缺不全的情况下创造性的平面设计也能够保留它们的识别性。兰德经常在他的企业形象设计作品中履行这一测试。

兰德为专业人士留下了巨大的遗产。在他生命的最后10年间，他出版了三本重要的书：《保罗·兰德作品集》（1985年）、《设计与本能》（1994年）、《从拉斯克斯到布鲁克林》（1996年）。不只是回顾，这些书的编纂遵循了他职业生涯奉行的原则。

第17课 雷蒙德·罗维——促进产品销售的人

雷蒙德·罗维于1893年11月5日生于巴黎，1986年7月14日在摩纳哥逝世，被看作是20世纪美国最著名的工业设计先锋。他的创作具有简洁、功能性、品质上佳、优雅的共同特征。无数的日常生活用品、交通工具及各种标志都是他的作品，直到今天，传奇的S1发动机的设计被视为标志性的经典设计和流线型的完美例子。

雷蒙德·罗维在夏普达尔高中开始工程学课程的学习，1914年因为第一次世界大战而不得不中断学习。战后他移居到美国，他的第一个也是仅有的受薪工作是为萨克斯第五大道百货公司和梅西百货公司的橱窗进行装饰设计。

直到1929年他靠担任时尚杂志的自由插画师来赚钱。尽管受过工程师的培训，这份工作正好将他的时尚感他作为工程师的培训结合起来。终于，在1929年他成为西屋电气公司的艺术总监并很快成立了自己的事务所，在这里他作为一个工业设计师创立了自己传奇的职业生涯。

"当两个产品在价格、质量、功能上同等时，外观好的将更畅销。"雷蒙德·罗维证明产品的成功不仅依赖功能而且依赖外观。他说："设计的目的是为了销售。"他还补充说："说得再明白一点，我知道最可爱的曲线是销售曲线。"

1930年左右开始的全球性经济危机的前几年并不好过，他的第一份工作是重新设计复印机。这是一台难看的复印机，是那个时候典型的制造业产品。事实上，它的构想仅仅只是为了履行复印的目的。罗维明白机器笨拙粗陋的构造不仅有潜在的危险性而且存在视觉和功能上的缺陷，尤其是伸出来的纤细腿部是拙劣的工业设计的典型。因此，他很快绘制了一张草图，显示出存在于这个笨重物体上的绊脚石，这样所有的文件快速运转起来。这似乎已经说服了客户。

1930年他的汽车设计梦想转化为行动的机会来了。赫普汽车公司的汽车销售低迷带来一场变革，极端先进的汽车设计似乎是操控这次危机的好方法。因此，当时的经济形势帮助还不怎么出名的罗维受到委托，设计新一代的霍普莫比尔汽车。1932年霍普莫比尔汽车的设计表达出朴实、简洁的美学概念，非常光滑和平坦的外形暗示着速度和运动，这就是后来众所周知的流线型风格。流线型风格的最大特征就是给人以速度感的封闭的流线型的外观，是时代活力的象征。

雷蒙德·罗维还作为设计顾问，为无数公司创建了企业形象。从1935年，罗维接到为好几个大型百货公司重新设计的委任。为好彩香烟和可口可乐设计新包装，以及壳牌石油的标志，著名的可口可乐瓶是罗维设计的代表。罗维说："可口可乐瓶是世界上设计最完美的包装。"他在1954年重新设计了这一著名的瓶子，他对那个独特图像的贡献是使已有的版本更苗条，赋予它更精致的轮廓，使得它对年轻一代更具吸引力。

20世纪60年和70年代，罗维作为美国政府的顾问，重新为约翰·肯尼迪总统设计了空军一号飞机。他考察了美国宇航局空间站的内部空间，评估了宇航员1969—1972年在其中的生活质量。雷蒙德·罗维的设计理念缩写为MAYA（极度先进，却为人所接受），是确保他如此多的设计得以成功的主要因素。雷蒙德·罗维1951年出版的自传《精益求精》是国际畅销书。

第18课　弗兰克·劳埃德·赖特和他的建筑

相信"建筑物的内部空间是建筑物的主体"的弗兰克·劳埃德·赖特（1867—1959）是20世纪最多产和最有影响的建筑师之一。从他早期的草原风格的住宅，到纽约古根海姆博物馆的雕塑曲线，他所定义的北美风格建筑有丰富的情感和对环境的敏感性。

作为北美现代建筑的创始人之一，赖特接受了新的技术、材料和工程技术，创造了20世纪最有影响力的标志性建筑。在漫长而多产的70年职业生涯中，他设计了1 000多个建筑，其中400多个得以建成。

赖特生于1867年，是威廉·罗素·卡里·赖特和安娜·劳埃德·琼斯·赖特的长子，父亲是一个传教士和音乐教师。他的父亲使他产生了对音乐的热爱，但是是他的母亲鼓励他成为一名建筑师。除了在他卧室的墙上挂上教堂的照片，她在一次对1876年费城美国独立百年博览会的参观时给他买了一套弗里德里希·福禄贝尔的幼儿园教学教具。这套教具由一组彩色带纸、二维几何网格和一组由立方体、球体、锥体组成的积木构成。后来赖特写了："枫木块……这一天一切都在我的手指中。"这些几何形状无限的、好玩的组合给予赖特建筑的核心形式。

18岁时，赖特进入麦迪逊威斯康辛大学学习工程学，但是，为了不顾一切地追求自己的建筑事业，他退学并搬到芝加哥。在那儿他很快在约瑟夫·莱曼·希尔斯比的建筑公司找到工作。然而赖特的雄心很快使得他来到芝加哥最革新的建筑师阿德勒和沙利文身边。路易斯·沙利文对赖特具有重要影响，让他负责公司的住宅建筑工作。他还在1889年给赖特一笔贷款来购买土地，在芝加哥的橡树公园地区为他和他的新婚妻子凯瑟琳·李·托宾建立一个家。1893年由于赖特接受太多的私人工作被要求离开公司。26岁时，他开始了自己的事业。

在接下来的16年，赖特在芝加哥特别是在橡树公园的大量私人住宅设计委托中发展出草原风格建筑。赖特的绝大多数客户非常满意他建造的房屋。这一点，使他名声大振。他极少发表的成就之一在于他对室内环境的掌握，特别是对照明、供暖、气候的控制。草原风格旨在创造真正的北美建筑，但是赖特也从欧洲获得灵感：法国理性主义作家尤金·维奥莱·勒·迪克的作品和英国工艺美术运动，他还对日本艺术及建筑和前哥伦布时期的美国文化了解甚多。

1906年，芝加哥的罗宾别墅是赖特最成熟的草原风格建筑。弗雷德里克·罗宾，一名工程师兼企业家想要一个充满阳光、看到街景的房子，但是他的邻居不能看到内部空间。赖特用砖块、混凝土、钢筋和玻璃构建了一个巨大的西面悬臂式的住宅，给予客厅隐私性并躲避阳光的照射。它抛弃了传统房屋紧凑的箱型结构，扩展了房屋空间，使用长条状的米黄色石头做墙基和墙顶，用红砖做墙面创造出低矮的、水平的舒展的建筑形式。中央壁炉在壁炉架上方开放，给了被赖特视为家庭生活的中心的客厅和餐厅更大的统一的空间。虽然没有户外花园，赖特使用大量的花盆、花架和花缸淡化了建筑的尖锐边缘，在每个平面上设计了平台屋顶、阳台或门廊以打破内部和外部空间的界限。所有的室内细节包括家

具、灯具、地毯和必不可少的艺术玻璃都是由赖特设计的。

这个时期赖特大多数的住宅设计委托来自于中等收入的专业人士，如教师和记者，以及一些像弗雷德里克·罗宾这样白手起家的商人。到1935年赖特意外地受到埃加德·考夫曼的委托，设计位于宾夕法尼亚州米尔鲁恩镇的流水别墅，该建筑成为赖特最富想象力的住宅解决方案，也是他最著名的建筑之一。

弗兰克·劳埃德·赖特于1959年逝世，享年92岁。尽管在他的职业生涯中有停滞期和低谷期，他坚持设计和建造房屋达70余年。在他逝世后，他还有一个蓬勃发展的实践尚未完成。许多建筑师或许因为十年与众不同的作品被人记住，与此不同的是，赖特能够使他的建筑适应一个快速发展的世纪的不断变化的要求。他利用最新的材料和技术，从浇灌混凝土到地板供暖，而且很高兴为各阶层的人设计。他也是一个用情感来工作的浪漫主义者。在核心空间有壁炉的一所房子对于一个家庭来说是近乎神圣的地方，事实上正是他的浪漫情感和情绪在建筑上和环境上的反映，使赖特的工作在今天看来特别具有重要意义。

第19课　时尚女王——可可·香奈儿

"潮流稍纵即逝，而风格永存。"

——可可·香奈儿

布里埃尔·邦思·香奈儿是法国时装设计的先驱，她的现代设计理念、从男装获得灵感的服装时尚、追求简洁的奢华使得她成为20世纪时尚界的重要人物。她是世界著名时尚品牌香奈儿的创始人，她对时尚的杰出影响力使得她在美国《时代周刊》评选的20世纪100个风云人物中成为该领域的唯一上榜人物。

香奈儿于1883年8月19日出生于法国的索米尔小镇，是阿尔伯特·香奈儿和珍妮·德沃勒的第二个女儿，在她出生时她的父亲和母亲分别是市场的小摊贩和洗衣工。她出生的第二天医院的员工才宣布她出生了，由于工作人员不识字无法提供或确认姓氏的正确拼写，由市长弗朗索瓦·普瓦图写为"Chasnel"。这个拼写错误导致当香奈儿后来声望越来越高时，传记作者几乎无法追踪她的根源。她有五个兄弟姐妹：两个姐妹和三个弟弟。

1895年，香奈儿12岁那一年，她的母亲死于肺结核，后来他的父亲因为需要工作养家而离开了家一段时间。由于父亲的工作，年轻的香奈儿在罗马天主教巴辛修道院的孤儿院里度过了6年时光，在那儿她学会了女裁缝师的手艺。学校的假期是和省城的亲戚度过的，女性亲戚教可可能够缝制比修道院的修女们更多的花色。关于香奈儿的早期细节模糊，大家普遍认同的是香奈儿在进入法国多维尔市的一家帽子厂工作前就获得了制作女装和女帽的经验。她在一个赞助者的财政援助下，利用她制作女帽的技能在巴黎、多维尔和比亚里茨开设了商店。香奈儿是一个精明的女商人，善于公关，迅速扩展了她的事业范围，包括裙子、针织运动衫和配饰。

作为20世纪20年代公认的设计师，香奈儿创立了适合正式场合的休闲装时代，去除紧身胸衣，创造了穿着舒适轻松的户外服装，以宽松合身的服装解放妇女。她的风格是简洁整齐，符合实用的细节。

香奈儿的设计理念具有极高的原创性，不断借鉴男性服装的设计思路，在女装中结合了男性化的剪裁。她的西装剪裁线条流畅精确不强调曲线，保持着相当的个性，简单优雅。马裤、宽腿裤、运动衣和毛衣都被采用和改进。香奈儿开襟羊毛衫与经典直筒裙的协调搭配，成为可穿戴式分离的标准组合。

她的颜色主要有灰色、海军蓝和米色，加上更丰富更广泛的调色板上最明亮的色彩。香奈儿推出了广受欢迎的"小黑裙"，可作为日常穿着也可是晚装，和燕尾服一起在香奈儿时代成为时尚界的一种固定搭配，直到今天仍然流行。

香奈儿注重细节，将真宝石和人造宝石、水晶簇、珍珠串、华丽的宝石袖扣的创新组合加入到她的日装和晚装中，给她的简洁设计加入了出色的对比，建立了广泛使用服装配饰的声誉。1922年香奈儿5号香水的成功研制协助她度过女装帝国艰难的财政时期。香奈儿职业生涯的一个有趣的方面就是在二战时期关闭的时装店的重新开业，15年后，香奈儿在1954年她71岁时重新启动她的工作，重新引入香奈儿套装，外观采用较短的裙子和编织开衫外套，这形成她许多藏品的基础并成为一种标志。

香奈儿渴望个人和财务的独立，她对成功的追求非常坚决，她在时尚界对服装的革命性改革及促进妇女解放方面是独一无二的。她的影响力触及了许多美国和欧洲的设计师，继续强化她的简单经典的概念。这样的设计师如卡尔·拉格斐在1983年接管香奈儿的女装生产线，来年它就成为高级成衣的总汇，他采用香奈儿的设计并做出调整，使它们吸引年轻的客户，将香奈儿带回了时尚前沿而广受赞誉。

第20课　宫崎骏的电影世界

宫崎骏出生在东京文京区的曙町，在四兄弟中排第二。第二次世界大战期间，宫崎骏的父亲宫崎胜治在他兄弟（宫崎骏的叔叔）开的宫崎飞机制造厂担任主管，生产A6M零式战斗机的方向舵。在此期间，宫崎骏画了很多飞机并发展出对飞机的终身迷恋，飞机成为他以后的电影中反复出现的主题嗜好。

宫崎骏的母亲酷爱阅读，经常质疑社会公认的准则。后来宫崎骏说他是从母亲那继承了怀疑的态度和质疑的思想。他的母亲从1947年至1955年间接受脊柱结核的治疗，因此经常举家搬迁。宫崎骏的电影《龙猫》就是以那个时期为背景，并以住院的母亲为家庭特征。

宫崎骏进入丰多摩高中，高中三年级时他看到一部电影《白蛇传》，该电影被誉为"日本有史以来第一部长篇彩色动画片"，正是这个时期他开始对动画产生兴趣。然而，为了成为一名动画片制作者，他不得不学习绘画人物形象，因为他以前的绘画都是局限在飞机和战舰中。

高中毕业后，宫崎骏进入学习院大学学习，1963年他从大学毕业获得政治经济学学位。他是"儿童文学研究会"的成员，是"那时最接近漫画的社团了"。

1963年4月，宫崎骏在东映动画得到一份工作，在动画片《汪汪忠臣藏》中担任中间画动画师的工作。在他到来后不久，他成功领导了一场劳动纠纷，1964年成为东映动画劳工协会的秘书长。

作为东映动画制作的《格列佛游记》的中间画动画师，宫崎骏首次获得了承认。他后来作为首席动画师、概念艺术家和场景设计师在1968年的《太阳王子》中起到了重要作用。该电影是由高畑勋导演的一部具有里程碑意义的动画电影，宫崎骏在接下来的30年里继续与他保持合作。

1971年，宫崎骏离开东映动画来到A动画制作公司，他在那里和高畑勋共同执导了六集系列动画《鲁宾三世》的第一部。然后他和高畑勋开始系列电影《长袜子的皮皮》的前期制作，绘制了大量的故事板。然而，在前往瑞典研究该电影并会见原著作者阿斯特里德·林德格伦后，他们被拒绝获得完成该项目的权限，这个企划最后被取消了。

宫崎骏的下一部电影是《风之谷》，是一部冒险电影，该电影的很多主题在他后来的电影中再次出现：对生态的关注和人类对环境的影响、对飞机和飞行的迷恋、和平主义。这是由宫崎骏编写并导演的第一部电影，改编自他的同名漫画系列，早在两年前他就开始了写作和动画绘制，但是直到电影发行了以后漫画还没有全部完成。

继《风之谷》的成功，宫崎骏和高畑勋于1985年共同创办了动画制作公司吉卜力工作室，通过该工作室他制作了几乎他后期的全部作品。

宫崎骏通过他接下来的三部电影继续获得认可：《天空之城》（1986年）讲述了两个孤儿寻找一个神奇的悬浮在天空中的城堡岛的冒险故事；《龙猫》（1988年）讲述了两个小女孩的冒险和她们与森林精灵的互动故事；《魔女宅急便》（1989年）改编自角野荣子的小说，讲述了一个城镇小女孩离开家园成为城市魔女的故事。通过这些影片，从《天空之城》中海盗的飞行船到《龙猫》中龙猫汽车在空中飞行，再到琪琪的飞行扫帚，宫崎骏对于飞行的迷恋是显而易见的。

1997年的《幽灵公主》重新回到《风之谷》的生态和政治主题，《幽灵公主》以宫崎骏最暴力的电影之一而著称。该电影在日本获得巨大的商业成功，是日本有史以来最卖座的电影，直到后来《泰坦尼克号》的胜出，并最终获得了日本电影金像奖的最佳影片奖。宫崎骏在执导完《幽灵公主》后退休，这在后来被证明只是暂时性的退休。

《幽灵公主》是宫崎骏的第一部用计算机绘图的电影，恶魔蛇是计算机生成的，阿西达卡是计算机和手绘的合成。虽然从《幽灵公主》开始使用计算机生成图像，宫崎骏在整个动画过程中使用传统动画制作方式。他在接受《金融时报》采访时说道："保持手工和计算机工作之间的恰当比率对我来说非常重要，我现在已经学会了那种平衡及如何使用两者，仍然可以将我的电影称为二维电影。"为了满足发行期限，《幽灵公主》首次部分地使用了数字绘图，这被用来作为以后电影的标准。然而，在他2008年的电影《悬崖上的金鱼姬》中，宫崎骏又回到了手工绘制一切的传统动画上，他说："纸上手绘是动画的基础。" 吉卜力工作室的计算机动画部门在《悬崖上的金鱼姬》开始制作之前已经解散，宫崎骏决定坚持手工绘制动画。

第4单元 中国艺术

第21课 中国山水画艺术

唐代晚期，中国山水画演变成一个独立的流派，是文人雅士逃避尘世、渴望与大自然水乳交融的具体表现。这些画作可能还传达了特定的社会、哲学或政治信念。随着唐朝的瓦解，隐退山林的思想成为诗人和画家的重要主题，面对人类秩序的失败，文人们寻求自然世界的永恒，隐退到山林中寻找避难所以逃避王朝瓦解的混乱。

宋代早期，对自然的想象和幻想成为井然有序状态的隐喻。与此同时，个人隐遁的画作在一个新的文人士大夫阶层中如雨后春笋般涌现。文人士大夫们颂扬自我修养的高尚品德，常常是对政治生涯挫败或事业不满的一种回应，他们作为文人学者的身份是通过诗歌、书法及一种以自我表达为目的书法般笔触的新的绘画风格得以确认的。这些文人士大夫所创造的老树、竹子、石块及退隐的黑白物象成为他们品质和精神的象征。

在元朝时期，当许多受到教育的汉人被禁止入朝为官时，被剥夺公民权利的精英们将他们的住所变成文学集会及其他文化活动的场所，宋代的人文画演变成为成熟完善的主导文化。这些集会经常以画作纪念，不是以写实的手法描绘一个实际的地方，而是通过一个象征性的速记的方式，如可能是由一个简陋茅屋代表的住宅，传达出隐居世界的共同的文化理想。由于书斋和庭院被文人们看作是自身的延展，这些地方在绘画中常常来表达它们主人的价值观。

明朝期间，当汉人的统治得以恢复时，宫廷画家的创作回到传统，复兴了宋朝的隐喻方式，以井然有序的皇家园林隐喻政权。与此同时，明代的文人画家通过元代文人士大夫的风格语言追求着自我表达的目标。"吴派"文人画的创始人沈周，在受各国文化影响的苏州城从事创作，他杰出的伙伴文征明被视为明代文人理想的典范。两人都选择闲居家中而不愿出仕为官，修身养性，终其一生重新诠释元代文人画家的风格。

清朝初年，许多明末遗民虽然过着退隐生活却矢志不渝，因此，清代文人画道德上的隐逸之风仍然保持着一种强烈的政治象征。往往由于无法接触到以前大师的重要画作，明末遗民文人画家们的灵感来自于当地景色美丽的自然风光。

自然物象至今仍然是艺术家重要的灵感来源。随着人类几千年的迁徙改造，中国山水发生了改变，但是中国艺术表现被自然界的形象打入深深的烙印。观看中国山水画，很显然，中国人对自然的描绘极少是对外部世界的表达，相反，它们是艺术家个人精神和心灵的表达，尤其是体现艺术大师们文化与修养的文人山水画。

第22课 中国民间艺术

中国民间艺术是中国极其丰富的文化和艺术遗产的一个重要组成部分。中国民间艺术因其多样的类型、真挚的内容、丰富的生活气息、鲜明的地方风格及浪漫主义的艺术手法，赢得了国内外专家的认可和好评。

民间艺术家善于理解和描绘生活的全部内容，倾向于体现生活的节奏和韵律。依靠直觉、印象、记忆及生活经验和对生活的理解来抓住他所描绘的现象或对象的本质，从而使

艺术形象完全不同于原型。在艺术表现和表达方面，民间艺术作品率真、自然、灵活、生动、亲切。他们以迂回的方式生存，以特有的图像表达理想，以情感思考，以具象的方式表达情感，在简洁中透着巧思、粗陋中透着精致、拙朴中透着幽默。民间艺人还魔法般纯熟地运用着装饰、比喻、寓言、象征的方法。自古以来，中国民间艺术一直在寻求理解和呈现中华民族的崇高精神。它体现出中国人民不屈不挠的斗志和品质，展示出他们开拓新的发展道路的不懈努力。

民间艺术珍品云集，包含日常生活的各个方面，受到人民群众的喜爱。民间艺术最常用的材料是随手可得的普通天然物质，民间艺术家们熟悉人民群众的审美习惯，他们的生命意识是基于人民群众审美经验基础之上的。在创造艺术形式方面受到大脑的理性和审美法则的指导，其中的一些作品似乎是粗制滥造的，但是却表现出极大的智慧、创造力、简朴和纯洁，蕴含着深刻的艺术哲学。民间艺术作品不仅仅给予人民美的享受和娱乐，还有知识和教育。民间艺术家们自孩童时代就受到民间艺术的熏陶，当他们给老民间艺术家当学徒时，美的种子就已根植心中。他们对美的热爱是永恒的。

手工艺作为民间艺术的最大类，因其实用和审美价值成为人们物质生活和精神生活的完美结合。民间艺术诞生于心，它不是一成不变的，相反，因它试图不断满足人们的审美需求而稳步发展。作为中华民族的传统艺术形式，民间艺术是社会审美心理和艺术家审美心理的综合，通过它自身可触及的媒介得以外化。它将随着历史、社会和人们生活的进步而不断发展。

陕西民间艺术

黄河中游是中华文化的摇篮，中华民族的祖先自原始时代就在这块土地上生活和繁衍。在中国历史上，陕西在很长一段时间是国家的政治中心，以拥有全国最发达的文化艺术而自豪。西安是西周、秦、西汉、隋、唐和其他六个朝代的都城，时间长达1 120多年。丝绸之路由此开始向西发展，长期以来，西安与日本和韩国保持着经济和文化上的联系。通过丝绸之路，西安与印度、中南半岛、中亚、西亚和欧洲一些国家和地区进行经济和文化上的交流。它曾经是东方文化的中心。

在该省所发现的古代文物包括淳朴美丽的半坡彩陶、唐俑、雄伟威严的周代青铜器、秦砖汉瓦、汉代石碑篆刻、秦兵马俑、汉唐石刻和壁画，它们都是中国艺术的典范，是过去工匠们智慧和技能的结晶。

陕西民间艺术种类繁多，其中剪纸是陕西最具代表性的民间艺术之一。陕西剪纸历史悠久，源于中国古代文化的摇篮，在一代又一代人之间传承。民间剪纸过去往往是作为刺绣的图案或窗户的装饰。春节来临之际，在关中平原的房子和陕北黄土高原上窑洞的窗户上都装饰有剪纸。各式各样鲜红的剪纸贴在雪白的窗纸上，呈现出浓浓的喜庆氛围。同时，剪纸包含了人们的美好祝愿。

陕西剪纸被认为是既粗犷豪放又简约夸张的艺术作品。陕西省不同地区的剪纸都有着各自的风格,陕北剪纸看起来较简练、淳朴、充满活力,而关中平原的剪纸简练与细腻交融。它们似乎生动地叙说着中华民族的古老故事,拨动着中国人的心弦。

第23课 陈秉鹏——在设计中寻找平衡

"更多的技术不是正确答案,但是正确的技术可以帮助我们找到答案。"

——陈秉鹏

在过去25年里,陈秉鹏提出了很多棘手的问题。他一直被视为技艺精湛的设计师,花了大量时间思考人类和他们的行为、趋势和材料,以及如何将它们平衡,以获得更佳的设计。他的前瞻性思维远远超越时尚和美学,而是研究功能如何完善可以获得更多的赞美,并提高既定产品、服务甚至是整个系统(如公共交通)的用途。

作为一名工业设计师,陈秉鹏是坚定不移的,他仍然决心要了解不同的个体对设计是如何使用和回应的。作为一个设计师,他不断地思考关于如何确保所使用的工具和知识能跟上现今社会急剧转变的问题。

通过1989年在纽约创立的自己的设计公司ECCO Design,陈秉鹏以用户为中心的设计原则帮助越来越多的国际客户的业务得以改进。他的根本宗旨是设计师应该明智的负起调节人与产品、企业和社会、技术和自然之间平衡的责任,并最终为社会带来变革。

陈秉鹏出生于广州,在香港长大并接受教育。1976年毕业于香港理工大学并获得工业设计学士学位,然后来到美国,在美国一流的设计学校克兰布鲁克艺术学院学习。通过学校的学习经历,陈秉鹏能够与产品和人机工程学领域先驱者们合作,并从中获益,这极大地影响了他的专业实践和设计方法。作为一个发明家,陈秉鹏迷上了丰富人生的创意理念,使其制造了多个产品,赢取了多个专利。

他的顾问公司ECCO,是一家广为人知且备受尊崇的公司,成功地解决了跨国公司每一个主要的消费群体的需求,包括赫曼米勒、维珍、丰田、KEF、LG电子及联想。他创意无限,在他的设计作品中经常采纳突破性的全新理念,以这种或那种形式,设计出多个畅销产品,如十几个最畅销的椅子、手机、CD播放机、洗衣机、钉书机、办公家具、车内互动声控系统、冰箱、耳机和无数其他的东西。特别注意的是他为美国新泽西州公共交通系统中的多层轨道车所做的整体性的重新设计。

ECCO的设计理念超越以风格和偶像为导向的限制,寻找机会融入社会责任、生态敏感性和文化联通性元素,它加强了可用性需求、创新、有见地的创造力、突破性工程和诗意阐述,以设计出有意义的产品并获得经验。

虽然他手法务实,以设计作为商业和社会的工具,他的作品却被众多国际出版物刊登报导,同时被全球多个博物馆永久收藏。这包括伦敦设计博物馆、蒙特利尔装饰艺术博物馆、以色列国家博物馆、德国的慕尼黑国际设计博物馆以及纽约现代艺术博物馆。

ID杂志称陈秉鹏为美国40位最具影响力设计师之一,而《商业周刊》赞扬他为"举世瞩目的美国新一代天才设计师之一"。2007年陈秉鹏获选为美国十大最具影响力设计师时,*Contract*杂志亦有类似的称赞。2009年,他为Bug Labs公司设计了突破性的组合式硬件/软件移动设备,成就有目共睹,淘汰了一些来自电子游戏、学术界和电视界的世界知名的决赛选手,赢得了2009年的世界娱乐技术奖。

陈秉鹏是美国工业设计协会的活跃会员，对设计界贡献良多，包括为工业设计优秀奖和国际消费电子展奖的工业设计奖项担任评审。近年来，他专注拓展现代中国设计的范畴。2007年，他与赫曼米勒合作研发和设计一个以竹制成的现代工效学扶手椅，将传统工艺和计算机技术相结合。这个突破性的椅子激发了陈秉鹏进一步探索从本土文化遗产中提高设计方式的渴望，这种方式如今成为陈秉鹏设计策略的重要部分。2010年12月3日，香港设计中心授予他世界杰出华人设计师大奖。

第五单元　设计教育

第24课　伯明翰艺术设计学院

伯明翰艺术设计学院（官方简称为BIAD）是一所位于伦敦市外的英国最大的艺术设计教学和研究中心，隶属于伯明翰城市大学，是该校规模最大、最成功的院系。《星期天泰晤士报》公布的"2004年大学指南"将伯明翰艺术设计学院评为"艺术设计专业优秀"等级。伯明翰城市大学声称："伯明翰艺术设计学院的艺术设计学以22分（满分24分）荣获英国教育质量保证委员会的优秀等级，被授予良好的质量保证称号。"

BIAD的历史在历经各种演变中可以追溯到1843年。19世纪90年代，位于玛格丽特街的伯明翰艺术学校在爱德华·R.泰勒的领导下变得成熟完善。伯明翰艺术学校是全国范围内把设计引入到艺术设计教学中的引领者（在想使用的材料中而不是在纸上进行设计工作）。1890年，一个专业化的分校即珠宝学院在伯明翰的珠宝区成立。到了1893年9月，中央校舍扩建部开放时，教师员工们已经被委派到刺绣、缝纫、木版等专业领域工作，还创建了许多艺术实验室或车间，用于壁画、模型制作、木制品的实践指导。1901年学校委员会建议进一步扩展教学大纲，以包括彩绘玻璃、书籍装订和写作（论述和书法）。

BIAD的主要校舍和图书馆位于Gosta Green，就在伯明翰市中心的北部，毗邻阿斯顿大学。其他较小中心的位置为：伯恩维尔校区（视觉艺术中心、基金会奖和夜校所在地）位于市中心南部郊区；玛格丽特街校区（艺术系）位于伯明翰市中心旁，紧邻伯明翰中央图书馆和伯明翰博物馆以及艺术画廊；和维多利亚街校区（珠宝学院）位于城市的珠宝首饰中心。伯恩维尔校区的"国际项目中心"举办国际艺术展和演出活动，而Gosta Green校区是"用户实验室"所在地，是以用户为中心设计的专业化的研究和设计实验室。

五所学校提供了范围广泛的继续教育和高等教育课程和研究计划：美术、珠宝设计、建筑设计、时装和纺织品及三维设计、视觉传达设计。

珠宝学院是欧洲在珠宝及相关产品领域提供教育和培训的最大机构。课程类型广泛，涵盖从中学入门课程到博士学位研究课程不同的教育层次。

珠宝和银器（荣誉）文学学士

该学科不断发展壮大成为英国最权威的学科之一。它的优势之一在于它多样化的方法，没有一个"内部风格"，而是通过个体的个人哲学和发展方向鼓励个性的发展。

整个教学计划的结构鼓励实际操作技能和创新思维能力的发展。贵重金属传统技能和工艺的使用与对非贵重金属和非传统材料的探索相得益彰。这使得高级珠宝的制造与时装走秀珠宝、功能餐具及配件和谐共存。

对外项目和竞赛是课程的重要方面。除了海外合作与交流的机会，还鼓励与BIAD其他学科领域保持适当联系。最近学生取得了一些成就，包括几个欧洲的奖项和展览。

该学科的毕业生就业范围广泛，包括珠宝和银器设计师、设计师/制造商、艺术家/珠宝商、顾问和管理人员。每一年进入到硕士和研究课程的人数都有显著增加，研究生课程对那些追求教学生涯的人来说至关重要。

第25课　萨凡纳艺术设计学院

萨凡纳艺术设计学院成立于1978年，它是一个能够提供学位课程的专业艺术学院，这在佐治亚州东南部是首屈一指的。学院意在将美国和全世界的学生们吸引到佐治亚州进行艺术深造。1979年，拥有5名理事、4名工作人员、7名教员和71名学生的萨凡纳艺术设计学院开办了。当时学校开设了8个专业。课程设置的目标有两个：为学生提供优秀的艺术教育和实用的职前准备。今天，拥有多个校区和网络远程教育课程的萨凡纳艺术设计学院仍然不懈地坚持这些目标。

1979年春天，萨凡纳艺术设计学院购买和修缮了萨凡纳志愿者卫队军械库，将其作为第一座教学和行政大楼。这座建于1892年的建筑重大历史意义是被写入国家史迹名录获得认可，为了纪念两位创立者而命名的"Poetter馆"，至今仍在使用中。

萨凡纳艺术设计学院为有才华的学生提供职业生涯的准备工作，在一个具有积极导向的大学环境中强调关注每一个学生的学习。目标是通过有趣的课程、鼓舞人心的环境和相关教师的指导，发现和培育每一名学生的独特才智。

萨凡纳艺术设计学院是受美国南部院校联盟委员会认可的能够授予文学学士和硕士学位的私立的、非营利性机构。学校授予文学学士、艺术学士、建筑学硕士、文学硕士、教育学文学硕士、艺术硕士、城市规划硕士学位，以及本科和硕士研究生证书。建筑学硕士学位被国家建筑鉴定委员会认可，教育学文学硕士被佐治亚州专业标准委员会认可，室内设计的艺术学士被美国室内设计教育学会认可。学院还获得南卡罗来纳州高等教育委员会的认证。

班级规模小，使每个学生都有机会获得个别的注意。教员们在各自的领域都有杰出的背景。国际教师和学生来自50个州和100多个国家。作为第二语言课程的英语和专门的国际学生服务人员可以帮助国际学生适应美国的大学生活。

学院的价值观

为学生提供独特的教育和改变人生的经历。

展现每一个工作环节的卓越品质。

保持礼貌、真诚的大学环境。

不断成长，不断完善。

创新,注重成果。

促进团队合作精神和积极的"可以做"的态度。

多付出一份代价。

学院通过下述的学术部门提供了一系列的学位和课程:

建筑艺术学院

传播艺术学院

设计学院

影视、数字媒体和表演艺术学院

美术学院

基础研究学院

文学院